MEANT FOR MORE

*Create Your Dream Life,
Plan Your Path,
And Start Living It Now*

MEANT FOR MORE

Create Your Dream Life,
Plan Your Path,
and Start Living It Now

KRISTIN RATH

www.KristinRath.com

© 2016 Kristin Rath

Cover photography by Jill Rath
Cover design by Vraciu Andreea

ISBN-13: 978-1540410153
ISBN-10: 1540410153

This book is for all the Dreamers
who are meant to be Dream Doers.

TABLE OF CONTENTS

INTRODUCTION

What do I want out of life?
What makes me happy?
How do I find my purpose?
What path is mine?
How do I achieve my dreams?
I know I'm meant for more than this, but what?
Is this all there is?

If you're asking these questions, you've come to the right place.

There *is* a path to your dreams. You just might not be seeing it right now.

With *Meant for More*, you'll gain clarity on what you value and want out of life; visualize how its brilliance can play out; and have a roadmap for the continuous journey that is your life, with amazing stops along the way.

Most people skip a few crucial first steps when they set out for their dreams.

This book will guide you in using your heart and soul to create and explore your Dream Life. You must first identify *what* you want, *why* you want it, and *where* it can take you. These three questions are not answered with your logical mind. They must be answered with your heart and with your soul.

Once the *what*, *why*, and *where* of your desires are clear, you can work on *how* it'll materialize. You'll begin transforming into the person you want to be, and your life will take shape to match what you've focused on and are co-creating with the Universe. [*For the purposes of this book, "Universe" means the all-encompassing energy of our lives which extends beyond us and our planet. Some think of it as God, Source, a higher power— whichever definition we choose, we are part of the Universe as it is a part of us.*]

There comes a moment of *knowing*, which you will feel in your bones and the core of your soul. With this knowledge, your path is unshakeable. No one can take your Dream Life away from you.

Before finding my current purposeful direction, I'd traversed many winding trails searching for what I was meant to do and be—in the industries of entertainment, business, education, hospitality—without ever doing the necessary thinking, planning, and research on *myself* first. I was either:

1. Dreaming and hoping, but not taking massive and continuous action on it.
2. Constructing specific and measurable goals but hindering myself with limiting thoughts and beliefs, many of which were unconscious.
3. Setting out to complete massive goals before knowing if they were my true passion, not just a passing interest.

Does any of that sound familiar?

I could have saved myself and my family a lot of headaches, heartbreaks, time, and money if I'd read this book when I was a teenager. Or in my 20s. Or even in my early 30s.

Soon after, I hit my breaking point. I could no longer ignore my innate wisdom that I was meant for more than where I was headed. The pain of not reaching my full potential was greater than my fear of change and uncertainty. I stopped being content with my complacency and started getting brave. Once I could finally see that my need for more out of life was really about loving myself, I was able to take action.

This book holds the framework of what I have learned, discovered, and created on my most recent leg of my life journey. In my search, I experienced the miracle of finding guidance and help when I needed it. As a result, many mentors and teachers played a role, most of whom I have never met. Some of what I learned was just to direct me to the next step, while many other teachings I still draw upon today.

I recognize that my path is a dynamic, living, breathing journey. The principles and steps within these pages are what I wish I'd had from the onset of my self-discovery.

Upon reaching the last chapter, you will know where you're headed; you will hold in your hands a plan of action from which to begin.

What this book won't do for you is tell you what you should do or who you should be. That's something only *you* can decide. This is the most personal of journeys. And when you put forth the effort into your own discovery, create an actionable and measurable itinerary for your Dream Life, and are responsible for your own transformation ... well, there's nothing that can stop you.

This guide also won't give you all the answers. I certainly don't have them all, and neither does anyone else. Especially when it comes to *you*. The good news is that you already have many of those answers inside you. There's a wisdom we were born with that has been influenced by what we were taught, how we perceived our experiences, and what we believe is true. To find our own answers, we must examine these beliefs and shed the ones that don't serve us.

When you feel the purpose of what you want and where you're going—see it clearly and experience it in your mind, living as the person you want to be in your Dream Life—your every day becomes fulfilled and joyful and amazing. Your Dream Life is not far beyond you in the future. It's already here.

This book is for people who want a change in their life, who aren't content with their life as it is now. They feel it in their soul—there is something more for them out there.

At times, you may experience some discomfort because I will ask you to get honest with yourself. I will encourage you to look into those dusty, musty, cobwebby corners in which you've stuffed boxes of unused, unwanted, and nostalgic stuff. This is not therapy, per se, but it *is* a kind of personal exploration. I will ask you to get real and dig deep.

Make a commitment to complete all the exercises. Some may seem more meaningful than others, but please do them all. You never know which will impact you most. You might be surprised. I know I was during my own process.

I wrote *Meant for More* to share what's worked for me in the hopes that it can do the same for you. If you're lost, don't know what to do with your life, don't know how or where to begin ... I'm here for you. It would be my greatest honor to be your travel guide and contribute to your discovery, as my guides did for me.

I invite you to take the first step into the life of your dreams. Dare to dream. Plan the best trip of your life. Make it as colorful, brilliant, and fulfilling as possible. What better time to begin changing your life than right now? You've been looking for guidance. Here it is.

Welcome to your purposeful journey on the path to your Dream Life. Happy travels. I'm thrilled you're here.

Thank you for choosing *Meant for More*. I have created bonus materials that you can use before, during, and after reading this book. They include:

✓ Video welcome

✓ Audio introduction of the book

✓ 2 guided meditations you can listen to anytime to increase HAPPINESS and RELIEVE STRESS

✓ Companion worksheets, including a DETAILED ACTION PLAN for making dreams a reality

Claim your free bonuses:
www.kristinrath.com/meant-for-more-bonus-materials/

SECTION ONE: CALIBRATE YOUR COMPASS

1

WHERE ARE YOU NOW?

The ultimate value of life depends upon awareness and the power of contemplation rather than upon mere survival.

–ARISTOTLE

The first step in creating a better life is to have clarity on where you are in this moment. There could be many reasons why you picked up this book, but at the center of it lies one profound truth.

You want change.

Wanting more or something different doesn't necessarily lump you into the "unhappy" category—so if you're resisting the idea of it being reasonable to want more from your life, let me assure you that discontentment can actually be a good thing. Seeking more drives us to learn, evolve, and experience greater fulfillment. If we were always content, we'd never want to change.

Even people who do recognize they want change often don't experience it, simply because they are unaware of the core issues behind their troubles.

You have to know what you're changing before you can change it—and before it can be changed, you must act or think differently.

These first steps may not be glamorous—or at times, comfortable—but these are the crucial building blocks to your Dream Life.

So ... Where are you now?

Knowing your starting point will bring lucidity to your next steps. We're going to do that by checking your fulfillment in all the areas of your life, and then explore what's going well and not so well in each of those areas.

Your Life Areas

There are four main areas of life most people have in common:

1. Relationships—your interactions with others. Subcategories may include:
   - Romantic Partner
   - Family
   - Friends
   - Community
2. Career—what you do for money, or for free, to contribute to your profession or career goals.
3. Finances—the money we earn, save, invest, and spend.
4. Self—comprised of these subcategories:
   - Emotional Self—self-talk, belief in self, how you want to feel about your inner and outer world. Your approach to, and view of, life.
   - Intellectual Self—mental stimulation and engagement. What you want to learn.

- Physical Self—self-care, fitness, nutrition, energy level, vitality, physical and sexual needs and desires.
- Spiritual Self—faith, spiritual practice, connection to a higher power (whatever that means to you).

!!!!!!!!!!!!!!!!!!!!

Before we jump into your first exercise, here are some important notes for your journey through this book, as it relates to the exercises:

- It's essential that you are in a physical and mental place to get quiet and go inward. If you can do that with noise and action surrounding you, great. But if you need to eliminate distractions in order to concentrate, create an environment that supports that. Turn off your phone's notifications and sounds. Stay off Facebook. Put up a physical or virtual do not disturb sign!
- All the exercises in this book are *just for you.* You aren't getting graded, and you don't need to show it to anyone. Therefore, understand that it's to your benefit to be completely uncensored.
- Don't edit your responses and, most importantly, don't judge yourself. It can be hard, but try to be objective. The fact of the matter is, the more detailed you are now, the better your results will be. Your answers to these exercises now will determine the level of action you can take toward your Big Dream Life— so don't hold back!
- Don't confuse "being detailed" with "overthinking." Being detailed means recording all your thoughts,

lovingly pushing yourself to go deeper with your answers; overthinking means being critical of them. Let your answers flow from the place where you are now and write it all down.

- For printable worksheets and other bonus materials that apply to this book, visit www.KristinRath.com/meant-for-more-bonus-materials.

Preparation:

- Have paper and pen handy. Only use a computer if you know it's the only way you will do these exercises! In *Advances In Haptics*, edited by Mehrdad Hosseini Zadeh, it is shown that when you write with your hand, different areas of your brain are involved versus when you type. Zadeh presents studies which show that writing by hand is a more complex cognitive process, one that encourages deeper, more attuned thinking and expression, as well as increased recall. The main thing is to complete the exercises, so if you still want to use a computer, turn off all distractions, such as your grammar/spellcheck, any notifications, and your Wi-Fi!
- It's a good idea to keep all these exercises in one place, like a folder or notebook, so each is easy to locate and reference.
- I have included approximate times in which to complete each exercise so you can plan your sessions accordingly. I recommend using a timer with an alarm. Setting a time limit on your exercises makes it easier to get started and stay focused since there's an established end point.

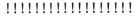

!!!!!!!!!!!!!!!!!!!!

Exercise 1: Fulfillment Check (Time: 3 minutes)

On four separate sheets of paper, write one of the four Life Areas at the top. For subcategories in Relationships and Self, list them in the margins, leaving space in between. So "Relationships" is at the top of one sheet, with subcategories such as Romantic Partner, Family, Friends, and Community spaced down the page; "Career" would be on a separate sheet; and so on.

[*For a printable blank version of the worksheet for Exercises 1 and 2, visit www.KristinRath.com/meant-for-more-bonus-materials.*]

Ask yourself how fulfilled you are in each area on a scale from 1 to 10, with 10 being "out of this world, can't imagine it getting any better!" (and really, if that's the case, why are you reading this book?) and 1 being "terrible" or "seriously needs improvement." You don't have to think too hard about it. Just write down the number that comes to you, next to or underneath each heading of Life Area and subcategory.

Exercise 2: Inventory List (Time: 20 minutes)

On each of your four sheets, divide the page into two sections by drawing a line down the middle. For one section put a plus sign and for the other section use a minus sign.

Ask yourself what's positive and not so positive in each page's Life Area. Below are some questions to jog your thoughts. Work through the pluses and minuses for one Life Area before moving on to the next.

On the positive side (+):
What are you happy with?
What gives you joy and fulfillment?
What makes you excited to get out of bed in the morning?
What are you proud of?
What do you want to continue?

On the minus side (-):
What are you unhappy with?
What's causing you pain and headaches?
What do you perceive as a problem?
What makes you want to crawl into bed to avoid?

Look at your results for Exercises 1 and 2. Do they bother you? Are you surprised? Are the things you listed on the minus scale important to deal with? If not, let them go for now. If they do need attention because of their importance to you, these are probably areas to focus on in order to achieve the life you want—highlight them. Either way, keep this list for later. You'll be using what you've learned here for future exercises.

By this time, you have a clear current snapshot. You've acknowledged your level of satisfaction across all areas of your life with the Fulfillment Check, and pinpointed exactly what is making you juiced or drained with your Inventory List.

Now it's time to dive into the commonly asked but crucial question that can cause anxiety or anticipation (or both!): *What do you want?*

2

WHAT DO YOU WANT OUT OF LIFE?

*The indispensable first step to getting the things
you want out of life is this: decide what you
want.*

–BEN STEIN

Congratulations on taking the first step to change: knowing your starting point.

The next step is to use your heart's wisdom to create and explore your Dream Life. This approach is necessary because our heads always want to be in the game. But when we allow our brain to come into play too early, we lose sight of what really matters—the purpose and the desire—and go straight to our need to figure it all out.

In an attempt to minimize uncertainty and failure, we skip over what we *want* to do and think about what we *should* do—what would be best for our bank account and family, what others and society deem correct or desirable—and proceed to build upon a foundation that doesn't exist.

Laying out the logistics and planning ahead is vitally important, don't misunderstand me, but first we must be clear on the *what* and the *why*.

This next question is a simple one that often remains unexplored and unanswered, eliciting unease when we can't answer with confidence:

What do you want?

Some people use blanket statements like: *I want to never have to work; I want to have nice things; I want be famous; I want to be a success.* These are valid and can be valuable to consider, but these answers aren't getting to the core of what the person really wants, at its essence. It goes much deeper than that.

If you truly want to make a change in your life from where you are—you have a clear picture of that now—and actually achieve the things you want, you must first identify *what* you want and know it on the deepest level.

The exercises in this chapter will help you understand what you actually want. Not what others want or you think you should want ... but what's deeply important to *you*.

Exercise 3: Your Heart's Desires (Time: 25 minutes)

Write down each Life Area and subcategories on separate sheets of paper as you did before. Review the answers you gave in the Inventory List exercise (Chapter 1, Exercise 2).

This time, ask yourself how you'd like those areas to change or what would make those minus signs become positive ones. What would you like to see manifest for you in those areas? In other words:

What do you want?

I have included questions to help facilitate your answers. This is by no means an exhaustive list of questions, so write everything you can think of. If you feel yourself stuck, ask yourself, "What *don't* I want?" Sometimes it's easier for us to identify what *does* cause us pain, discomfort, and worry rather than what *could* provide us joy, fulfillment, and peace. Write these "don't wants" down too. We'll deal with them right after this.

Some life areas will prompt many responses while others will not. Everyone is at a different stage; some Life Areas are more urgent or need more attention. It's the quality of your answers that counts here, not the quantity.

Remember not to judge your answers—lock those inner critics up!

Set your timer ... go!

Relationship wants:

- **Romantic Partner**—what qualities do you want in a mate? If you're in a relationship, what would you like to change, improve, or focus upon? How do you define a relationship in this category? What are your non-negotiables?
- **Friends**—do you want to create new friendships, repair old ones? What does friendship mean to you and entail? How do you want to connect with your friends?
- **Family**—do you want to be closer to a member of your family, or have a different kind of relationship? Establish boundaries? Spend more time

with them? What does family mean to you? Does it extend beyond bloodlines?

- **Community**—do you want to be more involved with your community? Why and in what way? Does community encompass your neighborhood, church/temple, online community, global community?

Career wants:

What do you want from your career? Does fulfillment rank higher than income? Or perhaps you can find fulfillment in other areas, like hobbies—then is job security most important? What environment do you want to work in—surrounded by others or on your own? Do you desire to work for a great boss ... or *be* the boss?

Financial wants:

How much money do you want to make? What are your material wants? Where do you invest your money, how do you save and grow it? Do you take riskier investments for greater gains or do you take the conservative route with less risk? What financial situation would make you feel safe and secure? What are your big financial goals? For example, it could be to improve your credit, buy a home, or save up for a vacation overseas.

Self wants:

- **Emotional**—do you talk to yourself with love, acceptance, and encouragement? Do you approach life with joy, calmness, confidence? Do you see that life is working for you and believe in abundance? Do you feel you have positivity and fun in your life? Are you focused and structured?

- **Intellectual**—what skills or information do you want to learn? How do you want to keep your mind interested and challenged?
- **Physical**—how do you want to physically care for others, and how do you want to be cared for? What are your physical needs—do you crave hugs and constant touch, or prefer less physical contact, or a particular kind? What does your sexual life look like? Does your nutrition need to change for better health? What would your most vibrant, energetic self look like physically?
- **Spiritual**—what fills your spirit and soul, gives you comfort in dark or challenging times? How do you want to grow spiritually? Do you desire more of a connection to something "greater than you"? Would you like to explore a new path or re-examine how you define spirituality?

Note for any "I *don't* want" answers: Before you read on, look for the opposite, positive qualities of those answers. "I don't want to be stuck in this crappy job" can be flipped into a "want" by saying something like: "I want to have a job that is stable, pays me well, and allows me off on holidays." Or "I don't want to be criticized all the time" can be flipped into "I want to be in a loving relationship in which I feel comfortable being myself."

Let's talk a little about your answers to the exercise. You probably have some awesome responses regarding what you want to have, do, and be!

The thing about what people say they want is, it's often not what they *really* want at the heart of it. We may not know that our true need and desire has nothing to do with our proclamation. When this is the case, even if we were to achieve the goal, we wouldn't feel fulfilled because we didn't get what we actually wanted.

Let me explain ...

Many people express the desire to be famous. That is not a goal in and of itself. Here's why: if you were to ask that fame seeker the reason they want to be famous, they might tell you, "I want people to know who I am."

Great. Why is that so important?

"Well, if I'm famous, people who were mean to me or didn't believe in me in the past will see I'm important and successful, and they'll know they were wrong."

If questioned further as to the significance behind that statement, the person might reveal: "If I can show others I made it, then *I will* know I've made it."

If pressed to answer why "making it" is significant, they might say, "I want to be seen. I want to know I matter."

Here's the progression of what the initial "want" was to what the resulting "core need" was of the example above:

I want to be famous. → I want people to know who I am. → I want people to see that I'm important and successful. → I will know I've made it and I will be truly confident. → I want to be loved and cared for. → **I want to know that I matter.**

Can you see how the "want" isn't about the fame and fortune? It's about being *seen* and *valued*. So if this person were to do everything to become famous without understanding that what he or she *truly needs* is to feel significant, the life goal may go unachieved—or, worse, increase feelings of unworthiness from the complexities and stresses the road to fame adds.

Let's deconstruct another common "want." Suppose you've said: "I want to be rich."

Why do you want this to happen? Maybe it's so you don't have to worry about bills. Why? Because you want financial security. What would financial security give you? The freedom to do whatever you want, when you want it.

Therefore, in this scenario, the breakdown is:

I want to be rich. → I want to achieve financial security so there are no money worries. → I want to do whatever I want, on my own time. → **I want to be free.**

In this case, you want to have control of your time and schedule, and you can't do that if you are locked into a restrictive job just to pay the bills. It's reasonable to think that being rich will give you freedom—it can—but there are other ways to achieve that core need without being a millionaire.

Before we continue, let me clarify: there can be and are other reasons why someone might want fame or money. The purpose of the examples above is to show you that there's often a deeper need to an "I want" statement that often goes undiscovered.

Not all of your questions will produce profound answers. They may be qualities you admire or would like to see in your life. "I want a partner who is funny and

makes me laugh" is about your valuing humor and entertainment and realizing it's important to you.

However, if the importance of humor is using it to
evade the truth, or avoid getting hurt, that's something to
look at. The underlying need to make people laugh may
actually be about desiring acceptance and connection,
and not knowing how to do it without humor.

Listed below are some general values which you could
consider to identify your wants and needs:

Control	Power	Reputation
Recognition	Fame	Achievement
Excellence	Leadership	Humility
Generosity	Compassion	Kindness
Love	Peace	Harmony
Justice	Humor	Playfulness
Curiosity	Creativity	Adventure
Challenge	Loyalty	Trust
Respect	Honor	Loyalty
Honesty	Integrity	Truth
Logic	Wisdom	Intelligence
Beauty	Security	Stability
Self-Reliance	Safety	Freedom

Knowing what you value—and being able to articulate
what it means to you—is not only crucial for dreaming up
your most amazing life, it's critical across the board—
from everyday decisions, business/career moves, choosing
a mate or friends, and knowing what you want to teach
your children.

So ... it's time to dig deep and uncover the *real* wants
underneath your answers in Exercise 3, and what you
value most.

Exercise 4: Discovering Your Core Needs (Time: 10 minutes)

What do you *really* want? What do you value? What core needs must you fulfill?

From your "wants" list in Exercise 3, look at each one and ask yourself why you want it. What's the real end result you desire? Keep going with the "why" until you can't go any further. Write your answers in the margins, or on a separate sheet of paper.

If one of the core values in the list above works, great. Otherwise, come up with your own values. The list I provided is by no means complete!

Did you have any revelations? Surprises? Once you get to the root of your wants—what you value—you can understand that your life can go various directions while still giving you your core need. For example, wanting your time to be your own can show up in alternate forms. There are many industries, jobs, and types of people who are able to say they dictate their schedule and what they do with their time. It doesn't necessarily take tons of money to achieve—and having tons of money doesn't guarantee your time is your own, anyway.

Identifying your core needs will be the litmus test in uncovering beliefs that don't serve you. Ask yourself if your want is something you learned from someone else, came from someone else's want for you, or was unconsciously adopted from life experience. Be curious.

Upon further examination, you might find that what you thought you wanted, or what you've been pursuing, doesn't match up with your core values because they are actually other people's history, wants, and needs and not your own.

You may be feeling confusion or pushback from this exercise. That's to be expected when you're rummaging around in your junk. Please be gentle with yourself, and remember to keep that inner critic silent.

Take a moment to recognize your important work. In this chapter, you've accomplished feats that a good number of people never attempt or even truly discover in their lifetime! You now have the awareness of what you truly want and value. This is a *huge* step and the foundation of creating your most fulfilling and joyful life. Seriously, give yourself a pat on the back.

We'll now proceed with shedding what's been keeping you from your goals and dreams—limiting beliefs and stories.

3

IDENTIFY YOUR BELIEFS AND STORIES

You don't manifest what you WANT. You manifest what you BELIEVE.

-Sonia Ricotti

In the previous two chapters you clarified your current reality and some qualities of the reality you desire to come to fruition. Your reality is shaped by your beliefs—what you know to be true about the world and your interaction with it.

Therefore, it's important to examine what your beliefs are, identify any that build a roadblock across your desired path, and replace them with supportive ones.

Exercise 5: Identify Your Beliefs (Time: 10 minutes)

If you were to sum up your personal perspectives and worldviews, what would they be? Below is a list of words that should readily produce responses. Your answers could be a few words or a sentence or two. Record on your paper the first thing that comes to mind. If you have several beliefs about the topic, include those too, even if they contradict each other.

As a whole, how/what do you believe about:

Money
Sex/Sexuality
Success
Strangers
Religion
Family
Men
Children
Different races
People in your hometown

Love
Power
Friendship
Meaning of Life
Spirituality
Jobs/Work
Women
Animals
People from other countries
People in your neighborhood

The following are some possible common beliefs about life and what effect they may have on the believer. Do any of these beliefs, or relatives of them, show up in your answers to the exercise you just completed?

- If it's too good to be true, it is. → Good things come at a high price. → Be suspicious of good things happening for you. → It's safer to reject gifts/blessings/ miracles.

- Love hurts. → People start out in love but end up hurting each other. → Love doesn't last. → Don't love anyone and you won't get hurt.

- Nothing good comes from change. → Trying new things is a risk and not worth it.

- If it ain't broke, don't fix it. → You have to wait until you hit bottom, or something is completely dysfunctional, before you can take action to improve or fix it. → Stick it out until you're forced to change.
- Just be grateful for what you have. → Don't complain or be greedy. → You shouldn't want more.

Do the beliefs you have about a particular area of your life support what changes you want to make there? If they don't, that's a cross-purpose.

Uncovering Cross-Purposes

According to the Merriam-Webster Dictionary, a cross-purpose is:

"...a purpose usually unintentionally contrary to another purpose of oneself or of someone or something else."

When your conscious wants are undermined by your (often unconscious) beliefs, you get blocked from what you're trying to achieve. You basically stand in your own way, limiting what's possible for you.

Let's take, as an example, a topic that carries a loaded and emotional charge for many people: money.

Much of what we think and talk about can be tied back to money: what you can or can't do, have, be; what you have access to; what kind of life you can have; how people look at you; what's expected of or feasible for you.

So let's say you want to be wealthy, and to you, that means having lots of money. This is a goal for many people, myself included. Money could make life a lot easier, right?

However, consider the issues with the following beliefs surrounding money:

- Money is hard to get and harder to keep.
- You'd have to win the lottery to ever have a chance at being rich.
- You have to spend money to make money.
- Money is the root of all evil.
- Money changes you.
- Money can't buy you happiness.
- Money brings misery.
- More money, more problems.
- Money makes you a target.

Do you see how these beliefs would hinder your goal to increase your wealth?

Additionally, you could have negative beliefs around the people who have money, such as:

- Rich people are jerks.
- Rich people think they own everyone.
- The rich use their money to control others.
- The rich get richer while the poor get poorer.

These beliefs come from the perspective that those who have money are "bad" people. If you think you are a good person and want to stay a good person—which I'm sure is the case—and ascribe to the above beliefs, you subconsciously stop yourself from ever attaining wealth because you don't want to be a bad person (a.k.a. a "rich person"). In this scenario, you've made rich people the enemy, tying wealth to a certain set of personality traits that you oppose.

Let's summarize this complicated cross-purpose. You want to have lots of money but:

- You don't think rich people are good people, and you don't want to become a bad person.
- The only way you'd ever get rich in the first place is if money fell into your lap.
- If you have money, everyone wants a piece of it and you'll either be taken advantage of or have to tell people (including family and friends) "No."
- Having lots of money will create a lot of change in your life, not to mention change your personality.
- Money attracts more problems and even if your life is "crappy," you at least know what kind of crap to expect.

Wow, being wealthy is such a drama and a headache! Why would you ever want to be rich?!

Well, you most likely wouldn't be rich—not while holding on to that cross-purpose. And if it did happen, it would probably be so uncomfortable that you'd find a way to lose it. Have you ever wondered why previously poor lottery winners blow their fortune in such a short time?

If you were to have these underlying beliefs about money and the people who have it, do you think you'd be supporting your wealth goals?

I used to have unsupportive beliefs about money. One was:

You have to work hard to be successful.

Success, to me, equaled money. So if I wanted to make money, I would have to be successful. And to be successful, I'd have to work hard. (Many people also believe this. Just stay with me a little longer as I explain.)

As a kid, my perception of success and making a good living was long hours, missing out on things, knowing your time wasn't your own, and tons of stress that keeps you from a good night's sleep.

That doesn't sound fun. At all.

Ironically, I did go on to "work hard" in many aspects of my life—school, sports, hobbies/interests—and achieved levels of success. However, all those achievements were unpaid. Therefore, they didn't fit the bill because, in my young mind, what counted most were the achievements you made in your professional life—you know, where you make your living.

Another unsupportive belief.

When I was in college, my belief affected me more prominently. I struggled with balancing work and play, afraid that high achievement would take away from a full and joyful college experience. I ended up with neither, as they were cross-purposes.

I certainly *did* want to be successful. I was raised to be successful in whatever I did, and it mattered to me. But my deeper need was *freedom*. What I really wanted was a flexible schedule.

However, I wasn't aware of my unsupportive beliefs and cross-purposes.

Around the same time, I became reluctant to take on too many responsibilities. What if I couldn't be successful in all that I did? Also, a packed schedule would eliminate any free time.

More beliefs that didn't serve me.

After graduation, things didn't get better. I unconsciously set myself up to fail or feel unfulfilled. Anything that resembled a stable 9-to-5 job was short-lived. The monotony of schedules and routines suffocated me. The perceived limited and lifeless trajectory of the job made me want to crawl back into bed. So I'd rationalize a reason to quit.

I unconsciously began finding evidence to support the belief that:

Success and money must not be for me.

I looked for attainable jobs that offered a more flexible schedule, but they didn't pay well. While it was a source of pain and disappointment not to achieve the success I'd been headed for as a teenager, I experienced a certain level of happiness that was important to me in achieving freedom of time.

To my detriment, I believed I had to choose between a well-paying job—that would give me financial support and future security but held my spirit and soul hostage—and a flexible job that was in line with how I wanted my life to look, but only paid enough to scrape by, and didn't have much room for advancement.

Yikes.

I had many stories revolving around money and success. There was the story that there must be something wrong with me. That I'd have to "suck it up" and take a job I was good at but didn't like. That I was destined to fall short of my potential. That I'd have to settle for an ordinary life. That my dreams would remain figments of my imagination.

Stories are what we tell ourselves and others to explain or justify what we see as our reality.

My stories didn't support a joyful reality or my desired future.

Do yours? What are your stories?

Exercise 6: What's Your Story? (Time: 10–15 minutes)

Part 1: Your "whole life" story.
If you were to write the story of your life in a nutshell, how would you recount it? If someone were to ask you what kind of life you've had so far, how would you answer? What would you say has happened to you? What would be the title of your autobiography?

Those who raised us were a huge influence in the formation of our view of the world and ourselves. Be on the lookout for any family stories you've taken on as your own.

Part 2: Your "now" story.
What do you say in a conversation, talking about your day/week/month/year? How do you sum up your current situation when you're reconnecting with friends or acquaintances?

What's the story you're telling yourself (and others) about the area of your life that isn't working? Is it a recurring story from your past?

Take note of any additional beliefs or judgments you find lurking in your stories, stated or implied.

Stories make up our beliefs, which make up our reality.

Do your stories encourage, inspire, and support you ... or discourage, disparage, and hold you back?

Are those stories True with a capital T? While each may contain facts, you most likely expressed a perception about it. You had an emotional response that colored the event one way or the other (i.e., this "bad" thing happened versus this "good" thing happened).

Once you've identified those nefarious "truths" and storylines ... what do you do with them?

How do you change unsupportive beliefs and stories? By finding evidence that they are FALSE and by proving that your supportive beliefs are TRUE.

Your brain will get on board with whatever you can back up with proof. One of its higher-functioning missions in life is to figure things out for you and offer evidence that what you believe is True with a capital T. So give your thinking center the highest-quality messages it can use to figure out how to make those wants of yours a reality.

Look for evidence in your history that proves that what you want is possible. There's always a way to disprove your unsupportive belief and find evidence of the opposite.

For example, if you've held onto the story that you aren't good enough, blast that story to pieces by recalling those times when you *were* good enough. Better yet, look for a moment you surprised yourself with how amazing you were. Every time you have doubts, pull up your highlight reel and tell yourself, *Well, that's not true. I'm obviously good enough. I have proof I've done it before, so I can do it again!*

What if you can't easily find evidence in your own life? **You can find your proof in others' stories.** There are people out there who have aspects of the life you want. More often than not, those people will have corresponding supportive beliefs.

Let's refer to my unsupportive belief concerning success: in order to turn around my story that wealth and success came at the cost of great sacrifice, I had to look for evidence to the contrary.

I found examples of people who are wealthy, highly successful, love their life, and dictate their own schedule!

Do those wealthy and successful people use a lot of energy and focus to live their lives? YES.

Does having that life end up in days where they work long hours? YES.

Does it mean that once in a while, these people miss out on something "fun"? YES.

But I viewed these discoveries as positive because they are making those choices to do what they love. And they get paid well for what they do. To them, it's not *hard* and it's not *work*. It's *play* with a *purpose*. And the purpose brings them wealth and success as a byproduct.

I always knew that I wouldn't achieve great things by sitting on the couch, dreaming of all the ways I could take action without ever doing any of them. But my beliefs that success and wealth were hard to get and required giving up a lot were sabotaging me.

I then realized I had a choice in how I perceived my goals. I could make up my own definition of what was True. I didn't have to take what others said—and was holding me back—as gospel.

It wasn't as if I couldn't find proof supporting my old belief about hard work. Many "inspirational" people perpetuate the belief that what is worth having and achieving comes only through Herculean effort. There's the famous quote from Thomas Edison about genius being 99% perspiration and 1% inspiration. I spy a great deal of hard work there. I could have found evidence with Theodore Roosevelt's quote: "Nothing worth having comes easy."

These well-known axioms, and many others, didn't inspire me to greatness. While they have served their purpose for others, they didn't work for *me* or toward what *I* wanted.

So I dropped them in favor of new, supportive beliefs that were high-energy, juicy, and made me smile. I repeated them, guided myself back to them when I slipped into old patterns of thinking, and took note of all evidence within and around me that supported what I wanted to see.

I chose to adjust my perspective, such as seeing setbacks as learning experiences; that there's more than enough time to do all the things that matter to me; that my desire to reach my dreams is stronger than my fear of failure.

When I put in fourteen hours in a day toward my goals, I'm tired at the end of it, but I'm also fulfilled. Again and again, I reaffirm that when I'm focused on my goals, it's not hard work. Instead, it's focused energy and intention. It's making leaps and bounds toward my big goals and dreams and enjoying the process.

You can experience that too. In fact, you are well on your way.

In the next chapter, you will step deeper into self-awareness by examining what you think and the words you use.

4

EXAMINING YOUR THOUGHTS AND WORDS

The world we have created is a product of our thinking; it cannot be changed without changing our thinking ... no problem can be solved with the same consciousness that created it. We must learn to see the world anew.

–ALBERT EINSTEIN

Although finding evidence that supports the beliefs you seek is an important component in shifting what doesn't serve you, there's more to it than that.

Something that might seem impossible.

To change your life, or an aspect of your life, **you must change your thoughts**. Why?

You are who and what you think.

Your thoughts are your inner commentators that are on the job pretty much 24/7/365. According to the Laboratory of Neuro Imaging (one of the foremost neurological research centers in the US), we have 60,000–70,000 thoughts per day, or about 48.6 every minute!

Your stories and beliefs are made up of thoughts you have over and over. So it's worth taking the time to examine the thoughts you have and recycle them.

I bet that in an area of your life that isn't working, your thoughts are unsupportive and limiting.

Your thoughts are the source of your suffering.

I repeat: **Your thoughts are the source of your suffering.**

I know it sounds harsh, but I said it—twice—because I want you to be aware of how powerful you are.

Picture a lemon. Imagine cutting it in half. Pick up a lemon half and hold it in front of you. Smell the lemon. Squeeze the juice into your mouth. If you've ever tasted a lemon, your mouth probably watered from recalling the sour taste you've experienced before. When you brought up the image of a lemon, your brain sent a signal to your salivary glands. The lemon wasn't even real! With a mere thought, you caused a physical reaction within yourself.

Your thoughts are powerful.

Now imagine what happens when you think self-effacing, destructive thoughts. Do you start to feel the emotions of anger, fear, or sadness? Does your body become hot, cold, or heavy? Perpetual negative thinking can take a toll on your body as well as act as a self-fulfilling prophecy.

Your brain magnificently carries out jobs on its own. But it will also follow what you tell it to do. You have this incredible choice to think in the manner you wish. You are empowered to throw a spotlight on undermining thoughts, shift them to supportive ones, and zero in on seeing those positive thoughts come to life.

You control your thoughts. What you focus on grows. You are powerful.

How often do you use loving, positive, nourishing words? Do you offer them to others but not to yourself? Do you gift them to yourself but not to others? Neither?

How do you talk to yourself?

If you do something you perceive as a failure or a mistake, what do you say to yourself? Is your response: *There you go again, messing things up. Why can't you do anything right? What's wrong with you?*

You might even play back an experience where a family member, teacher, or romantic interest told you you weren't good enough, weren't smart enough, or you were deficient in some way. You might even scroll through all your instances of failure; all the times you were humiliated you couldn't do it right; every frustration or fear of not knowing what to do.

Before you know it, you could be flying down a self-berating spiral and emitting a negative funk that can last the whole day. And it all started with a thought. A single, powerful thought.

Luckily, positive self-talk is just as powerful.

In the following exercise, you're going to take note of your objections in response to declaring what you want. You may have noticed some negative chatter already. These will be some of the thoughts that can hold you back, so you'll want to expose them now.

Then ... you'll crush them!

Exercise 7: Mind-Chatter Monitor (Time: 5 minutes)

Take out your answers for Exercise 3 and 4 (Chapter 2) on determining what you want. On a separate sheet of paper, write down your thoughts about them.

When you read over your wants, needs, and desires, what's the dialogue that goes through your head?

Write down as many thoughts as you can. Use exact wording where you can.

What kind of thoughts did you notice? Did you talk to yourself like a friend, or an enemy? Would you ever utter those comments to someone you love, respect, protect, and encourage? Did your thoughts look anything like this?

> *I can't.*
> *I won't.*
> *There's no way.*
> *It's not possible.*
> *It won't work.*
> *I'm not smart enough/rich enough/good-looking enough/thin enough/strong enough* [fill in anything else].
> *I could never do that.*

These are the types of thoughts you will have to stop and shift in order to achieve your dreams. Those thoughts are dictating what is possible for you. All the excellent work you do in dreaming up and planning for your most awesome life will have little effect if the sound-track in your mind is set to expect failure.

Be cautious of those words you use casually. If you break something and call yourself an idiot, your mind will say: *Ohhh, so you're an idiot? I'll remember that. I will support you, idiot.* You probably don't really believe that breaking something makes you an idiot, but if you say this enough, you'll begin to believe it on some level. You're brainwashing yourself to believe something you don't actually *want* to believe.

Whatever you say, positive or negative, your mind wants to support you. So give it the right messages.

Consider these common phrases and how they could be upcycled:

Life is hard, it's so complicated. → Life is an adventure.
I don't want/like that. → I prefer/choose something else.
I don't know. → I can figure it out.
Why isn't this working? → What would it take for this to work?

See the change in focus to what could be possible? Your mind will shift from pointing out all your pitfalls, potholes, and flat tires to seeing alternate roads paved with solutions and opportunities.

Upgraded messages take you from powerLESS to powerFULL. Bring awareness to how your everyday messages affect the creation of your future.

I think you can now see how important the quality of our thoughts are, especially when you're working to create the life of your dreams.

Thoughts you think over and over form your beliefs. Your beliefs shape your experiences, which form your reality.

Therefore, it goes to reason that if you want a better reality, you'll want to focus on better thoughts. Words make up our thoughts, so pay attention to the words you choose.

Advertisers spend a lot of time and effort nailing the right words for ads. They use the ones that will evoke the emotional response in the target consumer to buy the product or service they're advertising.

Why wouldn't we use that same care and consideration (and more!) to benefit our own lives? Choosing your words thoughtfully can create the emotional response in *you* that's needed to achieve your goals and what you want to experience on a day-to-day basis.

Pull up some of the thoughts you've had today. What was their flavor? Drab, uninspiring, scary, disheartening, abusive? Or were they juicy, loving, encouraging, fun? Do they lift you up or drag you down when you remember them?

Exercise 8: First-Class Thought List (Time: 5 minutes)

Look at the unsupportive thoughts from the last exercise and examine how you could upcycle them to supportive ones. For each negative thought, come up with the most supportive, loving, and happy thought possible to replace it.

Write each of these new First-Class Thoughts down on a new sheet of paper.

You might want to transfer your upgraded thoughts to a notecard, your phone's notes section, Post-it notes placed throughout the house, or somewhere it can be easily accessed when you feel low or recognize your thoughts are headed south. When you're trying to shift a negative thought you've been telling yourself—especially one you've repeated for years—it's going to take some reminding. Having your replacement thoughts handy to review throughout the day or week will help you make the shift permanent.

Remember my unsupportive beliefs about money and success shared in Chapter 3?

I thought success was HARD,
required LONG HOURS,
created STRESS,
and resulted in many SACRIFICES.

Just those words in all-caps alone had an effect on me, never mind the thoughts that were stirred up from feeling the weight of them in my body!

When I became savvy to how my thoughts and word choices mattered, I worked on replacing those energy-zapping, defeatist perspectives with energizing, wildly satiating viewpoints.

Now ...

I work SMART.
I use FOCUSED ENERGY.
I do the things that bring me closer to the juicy goal I
LOVE.

Smart. Focused energy. Love. These words make me smile. They provide a sense of ease and confidence. They support me in my goals.

Do I still slip up and have those moments of doubt, fear, and uncertainty regarding success? Certainly. But through practicing awareness, I can catch them before they cause me harm. I shift them to supportive thoughts. I basically talk myself off the cliff and back onto my purposeful path.

Your story matters. The thoughts you think matter. The words you use matter. It can be the difference between getting everything you truly need and want, and not achieving or experiencing those things at all.

You've done great work in this chapter!

Continue to monitor your thoughts and words. Don't judge yourself for unsupportive self-talk—that's adding on more negativity! Instead, guide yourself to a better thought. As you continue to shift your thoughts in the direction of positivity, the quality and strength of your thoughts will improve, propelling you toward your dreams from the inside out!

Speaking of dreams ... it's time to start creating your most awesome life and bring it into focus!

SECTION TWO:
CREATE YOUR
DREAM DESTINATION

5

YOUR BIG DREAM LIFE

*You have to dream before your dreams can come
true.*

-A. P. J. Abdul Kalam

Now that you've laid down a solid foundation to support
what you most desire and wish for yourself, it's time to
dream big!

Why?

The more clearly you can see *where* you want to go,
the more likely you are to get there. You need a destination in sight, something you can circle on the map—a big
"X marks the spot!"

We tend to undervalue ourselves and limit our
dreams. We are told to be realistic, focus on paying our
bills, prepare for the future that most closely corresponds
with how much we can save. While this advice is pragmat-
ic, it doesn't mean there isn't room for your dreams and
their fruition. You *can* have everything that matters to

you. But you need to plan for it—which we'll focus on in Chapter 8.

Before you do any of that and allow your logical mind to throw in its two cents ...

You're DREAMING BIG!

When you do this, you're going to hear some of these inner voices:

Are you serious??
Who do you think you are?
You want to do WHAT?
No one like you gets that life.
No one in the world has ever done that, so YOU certainly can't!

Hearing these voices is actually good—it means you're shaking yourself up with your dreams. Don't indulge the critical voices, though. Just take note of what comes up. Hopefully, you've already started to reign in those negative thoughts and choose positive ones. We touched on this in the last chapter, but I will show you more ways to do so in later chapters.

What would your life look like if nothing was holding you back? What would you do?

When I did the exercise I will ask you to do next, my answer was "*Heal the world.*"

Yep. Heavy stuff.

Asking yourself this question is a revealing and, sometimes, shocking experience. Imagine coming up with the essence of what you really want in your life, without all the bells and whistles. To strip it all down to one simple truth, directly from your soul's desire. I've witnessed someone else come to that moment as well. I never would have come up with my answer had I not questioned myself further, and neither would the woman I will now call Carol.

A friend of mine, Jai Maa (pronounced "Jay MAH"), is a faith minister, motivational speaker, and all-around goddess. She has led workshops centered on what she shares in her book, *Break Through Your Threshold: A Manual for Faith-Based Manifestation and Co-Creating with God.* A visit to my parents in Florida coincided with one of her events, so I attended.

During the workshop, Jai Maa asked us to think of what we would do with our lives if there was nothing holding us back. She asked for a volunteer to share his or her answer. A woman in her seventies, one row in front of me, whom I've renamed Carol for anonymity's sake, raised her hand. She didn't understand how she could answer the question. Many of Carol's family members were going through trying times, and the drama was affecting her emotionally.

Jai Maa nodded her head in understanding but asked again what it was that Carol wanted—what if she didn't have to deal with her family's dramas?

"I would go kayaking," she said, "but my back is in bad shape, so I would have difficulty with that."

Jai Maa smiled at her mention of kayaking. She asked Carol what else she would do.

"Oh, I don't know. I've never thought of what I could do if I didn't have to deal with everyone's problems." After some thought, she mentioned reading and relaxing.

"So what is it that you really want?" Jai Maa asked.

A long pause. "Peace," Carol replied. "I want peace."

Although all I could see was the back of Carol's head, I could feel the bare, undeniable truth of her answer. Jai Maa's eyes glistened as her face mirrored what I had experienced from Carol's soul speaking her truth.

"I never would have thought that's what I want," Carol said quietly.

And she never would have gotten to her *real* want in life had she not asked the question, shedding all her excuses that kept her in a state of stress—her family, her back—until she was willing to consider her life with no limitations.

We get so wrapped up in what we should do, what we think we can't do because of our problems, what material goods we need, what kind of person we wish we were ... but we never ask our soul what it wants, at the core of everything. The answer will be so shockingly simple to us, as Carol's answer was. As mine was. But the answer, however simple, must be honored, held with respect, and earnestly explored.

Carol's answer, while abstract and undefined, was a comforting beginning.

If she could step forward from that realization in the direction of pursuing peace, achieving peace, and remaining in a peaceful state—whatever that ended up looking like—she would be happy and fulfilled.

It doesn't take *thinking* to get to your core. What it takes is listening, getting quiet and still, and connecting with your highest self. This has a direct connection to Knowing and Receiving.

Remember my recommendation before the first exercise of this book? I suggested finding a quiet place to limit distractions. Now is a time when quiet listening is required, so if you haven't done so—find your spot.

Now, it's your turn to uncover your Truth. Truth with a capital T.

Exercise 9: Dreaming Without Limits (Time: 5 minutes)

Bring to mind all of those perceived problems you have. The ones that are bugging you, you're worrying about, you feel are thorns in your side, all of your perceived "inadequacies." Bring them all up.

How does that feel? Not too great, right?

Now ... imagine they all disappeared. *Poof!* Not an issue. There's no limit to the amount of resources you have: time, help, energy, health, money, education.

If none of your current problems existed, what would you do?

Write down the first few things that come to mind.

If you have all the resources, help, and knowledge you need, what could you do with your life?

Write down your answer.

Remember, nothing is impeding you! Money is no object; you are equipped in every way, every day. What would you do?

What will you do if there's absolutely no way you'd fail? If success is guaranteed?

Don't you dare judge your response—just write it down.

How did that feel? Weird? Awesome? Exhilarating?

Does your answer scare you? Is your mind running overtime with questions? Well, here's one more:

Why not do it anyway?

I know, I know ... *how* are you going to get from here to there, right? You say, "But my resources aren't actually unlimited. I'm limited! I'm limited!"

I had the moment you're going through now, too. But guess what? A momentous thing happened after my epiphany of wanting to "heal the world"—I started a ball rolling I didn't know was there. What I used to think of as only a possibility for others, I now consider possible for *me*.

You are going to gather your previous exercises that revealed your wants, core needs, and values and incorporate them into your Dream Life. After reviewing them, you'll write down how you want your life to be in a Big Dream Life declaration. You'll have a technicolor picture that you will incorporate later.

This is for you to feel *to the moon* about! If it becomes a chore, check in with yourself. Lovingly push yourself—but this is not about making you feel constricted and punished. Block out all those *hows*—we aren't interested in them yet. All of that comes later. For now, focus on the *what* and the *why*.

So let's get started!

Exercise 10: Big Dream Life Declaration (Time: 30 minutes)

Combine all the things you discovered as elements of what you want to add to your Dream Life into a Big Dream Life declaration.

There are several ways you can do this:
1. Write it all down based on each Life Area.
2. Take a typical day and go through from the time you get up to the time you go to sleep—or take several days or a week in the life and detail what would be happening.
3. Free write as you wish, in no particular order.

I like to put on some inspiring instrumental music and allow myself to daydream for ten minutes or so and then write down what I envision.

No matter which way you choose, remember to:
- Use the present tense (I am, I have, I do, My family is, My friends are, etc.).
- Make it as specific as possible; but if you get hung up on details, move on.
- Make it juicy! Add in anything you haven't explored yet, like Bucket List items or whatever would be fun to have happen in your lifetime.

Some questions to consider:
- How would you spend your day? Who would you spend it with?
- Where would you go?
- How would you show up in the world?

- What legacy do you want to leave?
- What are the adventures you want to have, skills you want to learn, achievements you want to make?

Turn up the color, sharpness, contrast, and intensity until it's blinding!

If, after this exercise, you're feeling really raw and vulnerable—as if you've just made a list of things you'll never achieve in your lifetime—don't run from it. That's a positive sign. Don't scrap it because it seems impossible. It doesn't mean it's not going to happen! Opportunities and resources will show up for you—and you'll actually recognize them—when you look at life through a positive lens.

Again, take note of what emotions, thoughts, and issues come up for you. As you peel back the layers to reveal your authentic self, you will encounter deeper-seated beliefs that have held you back.

Continue to work on releasing what's unsupportive in favor of what lifts you up. A way in which you can continue exploring your Big Dream Life comes next.

6

MEET YOUR FUTURE SELF

*People often say that this or that person has not
yet found himself. But the self is not something
one finds, it is
something one creates.*

–THOMAS SZASZ

You're going to meet and get really familiar with your
Future Self now—the one living that big, beautiful life you
imagined in the last chapter. In fact, you are going to *be*
your Future Self, starting today.

You might be wondering how this is possible, especially when your Dream Life is so different from your reality.

That's completely understandable. You see, we're often
taught we must *have* the thing before we take the actions
or *do* the thing, and then we'll *be* that person who lives
the life we want.

For example, if you're a confident, limitless person in
your Big Dream Life, you might think you have to *have*

confidence to *do* a bunch of things successfully ... and then you'll *be* a confident person. Right?

Wrong. Although you can get there that way, it's neither efficient nor reliable.

That type of thinking is: Have. → Do. → Be.

We're going to reverse it. As in, you're going to *be* the person, then *do* the thing/take action, and then you'll *have* the things you want.

That's: Be. → Do. → Have.

Your dream starts with you in present time—by being the person you see in your Big Dream Life.

How?

If you imagined yourself as a successful person, with great wealth, and having amazing experiences ... how can you possibly do that now? You don't have the success or the money. How can I expect you to be that person?

Here's how.

Let's take your image of Successful You, which many people see in their Big Dream Life.

[*The following aren't qualities all successful people have. But those who practice balance, joy, and gratitude usually ascribe to these qualities.*]

Successful people THINK certain things:

- They have supportive belief systems. Take money: they see it as a cool tool to get and facilitate what they want; it makes life easier. They see money as neutral, whereas most other people give it personality traits, reputations, and power. It's really a means of transaction, like trading sheep for grain in 6000 BC, except more portable and convenient.

- They respect money. They spend their money intentionally and with awareness (they don't fritter it away).
- They save and grow their money.

Successful people KNOW certain things:

- They know about investing—real estate, stock market—or trust someone who does.
- They stay on top of business and industry news.
- They have accessed their risks and strengths and taken action to minimize the former and maximize the latter.
- They know their financial numbers (profits, expenses, net worth, etc.).
- They know people. They see the value in connections with others and make the effort to cultivate relationships. So when they need help and guidance, they know who to call.
- They have supportive beliefs about abundance and manifestation, and know that if they make their intentions clear and take action they are likely to hit their goals.
- They know ignoring their problems will not solve them.

Successful people DO certain things:

- They practice discipline.
- They schedule what's important.
- They're generous because they know their life is abundant and they'll get it back in some way and exponentially so.

- They respect their own resources. This goes beyond money; it includes time, energy, health. They don't overextend. They know how to say "No" and stick to it.
- On the flip side, they don't take "No" for an answer. They're creative solution finders.
- They don't do what they aren't willing to do.

Aren't these things you could implement into your life immediately? So when you say you can't be a successful person now, I'm calling you out for trash-talking yourself. You *can* be that person you imagine in the future starting *now*—simply by thinking and taking action as Successful You.

You *can*. And remember, "can't" is a dangerous word to use on yourself. Take that out of your vocabulary.

There is *always* a way.

If you see yourself as being joyful and having loving relationships, being in a constant state of gratitude, enjoying the moment ... you can start bringing all of that into your life *now*. Although you may not have all the things you want and need in your present, you can enjoy those things you *do* have, *right now*.

If you think about it, there are so many people with "reasons" that have stopped them from their dreams. Multiple jobs, a family to take care of, health issues, money problems—any combination of them, or maybe all of them. Those are all valid. If you have these issues in your life, no one would blame you if you didn't reach your dream.

Would *you*, though? Would it be a regret with which you could make peace?

It's a given that life is full of adversity. What we *do* with the adversity is what makes the difference.

If there's a roadblock, it can be destroyed, dismantled, and moved. If there's a wall that you hit, there's a way to go around it, over it, under it, or through it. You might not see it in the moment, but there's a way.

The only thing that stops us is ourselves. When we create that roadblock and when we build that wall—and yes, we are the only ones who can do it—we believe it's there, that it has power, and that it's unconquerable. That's when we stop believing in our dreams.

No matter your obstacle, I invite you to see it only as a *temporary* one.

You're responsible for manifesting your dreams or leaving them behind. So take all of your excuses—get really familiar with them and all their ickiness—thank them for exposing your fears, and keep on going. Those excuses have no business stopping you. That doesn't mean they go away. Doesn't mean you live in La-La Land and are out of touch.

But ...

Your obstacles do not define you. They will not stop you. I won't allow that for you and neither should you. Be your biggest supporter. Be the person you desire and envision *today*.

The first time I took part in a Future Self visualization, it made such an impact on me, I just had to share my experience with my readers on my blog Words Are Food. I thought I'd include the main portion of my entry here, so you have a "first-timer" perspective.

January 13, 2010
Getting to Know Yourself ... In the Future

I met my future self a few months ago. No, I'm not crazy. And no, I didn't find a worm hole in the space-time continuum. It was an exercise given to me by my career coach.* I was to envision my Future Self, meet her, step into her body, and experience what her life felt like, then step back into my Present Self and ask her any questions I had for ... well, for myself. It sounds confusing and pointless when I see it written down, but it was far from it. It was one of the most liberating, inspiring, moving, and unexpected exercises I have ever done—and believe me, as an actress and self-help enthusiast, I've participated in enough of them to last several lifetimes.

After reaching a state of relaxation, I was led through a series of visualizations that took me from the Meta Center in New York City on September 9, 2009, to a serene, white sand beach on the California coast (my choice) twenty years later.

I was asked to envision and observe myself in every-day life. My Future Self was completely confident, at ease with the world, at peace with herself, and was such a beautiful and inspiring person to watch. When I stepped into my Future Self, I literally felt different. The distinction between my two selves was tangible and dramatic. Tears ran down my face because I was so happy for my Future Self, and my Present Self could see how great it was to feel that way. It's one thing to imagine the way you want to be and feel. It's completely different to *actually feel it and experience it as yourself.* Honestly, it was a little freaky, even for me. After returning to my Present Self, I had the opportunity to ask my Wiser Self advice. And wise she was. I also received a gift from future me. It was a palm-sized, golden heart, which faintly glowed as if lit from within. I have no idea what significance it had but it was a lovely gesture nonetheless. After we said our goodbyes, my coach led me back to present time and space. I felt rested, rejuvenated, and optimistic toward the future. I might not see a clear path to where I want to be, but I feel confident that if I continue to believe in my talent, keep taking action toward my goals, and stay true to myself, I will eventually reach my destination.

*Melissa Rosati, listed in Resources section of this book

The following exercise combines a few Future Self visualizations I have done since then. This kind of visualization works best as a guided audio, but the format here still has value. Just read through the directions before beginning, so you know what the process is. Make sure you're in a place you won't be disturbed.

Ready to meet your Future Self?

Exercise 11: Your Future Self (Time: 20 minutes)

Reread what you wrote for your Big Dream Life Declaration (Chapter 5, Exercise 10) and scan it for any details of your Future Self to make those fresh in your mind:

- What do you look like, sound like, feel like?
- Who do you surround yourself with?

- How do you interact with others?
- What do you think?
- What do you know?
- How do you see the world?
- What is your approach to life?
- What are your beliefs?
- What kind of person are you?

If you don't have all those details, don't sweat it. You can explore those more here.

With your eyes closed, call up a portion of your Big Dream and jump in. Do you see yourself in your dream as another person, or are you experiencing it through your own eyes? If it's not first-person perspective yet, ask yourself to step into the self who is living that dream.

Then ... take the step.

As you see aspects of your Big Dream play out, concentrate on the feelings you have in that experience. How would your Future Self feel? How do you feel *as* your Future Self? What wisdom does your Future Self hold that would benefit you today?

Feel the happiness, sense of peace, deep love for yourself and others, and confidence. Experience the gratitude for all you have and are and the joy of living life to its fullest and highest potential.

Allow your dream to take you where it will, bringing awareness to how you feel in that future.

How was that for you? I hope you're feeling excited to start living your visualization!

You won't transform into your Future Self tomorrow—but you will *be* your Future Self today! When you start being that person, you're setting things in motion. Imagine how great it will feel to take a more supportive, loving action instead of sabotaging yourself like you once did.

Make a better choice than you did yesterday, and continue those better choices today, tomorrow, the day after ... It adds up, and it makes a difference.

Don't wait to be happy. Be happy *now*.

Don't wait until your life is full. Be fulfilled *now*.

Don't wait for love. Be love *now*.

The more you can be your Future Self, the quicker your future will happen for you.

Now that you have a good sense of the power of visualization, I'm going to show you some tools for solidifying and strengthening your Big Dream.

SECTION THREE: CHART YOUR COURSE

7

AFFIRMATIONS AND VISION BOARDS

I am not what happened to me,
I am what I choose to become.

–CARL JUNG

In Chapters 3 and 4, I discussed how powerful your beliefs, stories, thoughts, and word choices were in creating
the reality you want to see. In Chapters 5 and 6, you
started to unleash your wildest dreams and imagine the
You that is possible. In this chapter, I am introducing
two tools you can use to support your journey so far, as
well as in the future.

One is...

Affirmations

You may have heard of affirmations before–it's one of
the buzzwords in the personal transformation arena.
However, affirmations are only useful if you understand

what they are, what they can do for you, and how to utilize them.

Affirmations are not merely statements declared with conviction. Affirmations are used to focus your intentions (what you want to see happen) and encapsulate the feeling of achieving those wants. They can help when you're feeling unfocused and defeated by reminding you of your *what, why*, and *where.*

In the beginning, you'll want to incorporate your affirmations daily so they become habitual. Just like the other skills you've learned here, it's not a one-and-done activity. Using affirmations on a regular basis can center you and help manifest what you want in your life. Over time, they create a type of mental muscle memory and you start integrating the messages into who you are.

How to create powerful affirmations

Use present tense.

Starting an affirmation with "I will ..." puts you in the future, and will keep what you want in the future! Using present tense–"I AM ..."–brings what you are doing and how you see the world into the moment.

Many of your affirmations will start with "I AM ..." Keep in mind that this a powerful expression; you are declaring who you are. Be aware of the message that follows. Only use supportive, loving words. (Also keep it "I AM" instead of "I'm" or "I am" because it's a signal of a power statement.)

Stick to positive words.

Remember the exercise listing your wants (Chapter 2, Exercise 3)? If you were stuck, I encouraged you to first think of what you didn't want, then asked you to flip it into the positive of what you *did* want. The reasoning behind that is what your mind focuses on grows and those things show up more for you. If words like "no," "can't," "don't want," and "never" generously pepper your thoughts, your mind will zero in on negative aspects of your life. Positive or negative, if you look for either one, you'll seek it out and find it!

Bring what you "want" closer to you with upgraded vocab.

Until this point, I have asked you what you *want* because that's the easiest way to tackle your identification of desires. You're now at a more advanced level, so we're going to drop that phrase. Why? Because saying "I want" is not the strongest expression. More powerful substitutions are:

I AM accepting.
I AM receiving.
I AM attracting.
I AM manifesting.
I AM welcoming.
I AM excited about this coming into my life!

Don't those phrases feel more immediate? Like your goals and desires have already arrived and are waiting for you?

Make them believable.

Your brain needs to be able to get on board with what you're saying, or at the very least, its possibility. Otherwise, your affirmation will invite in your snickering peanut gallery (your inner critic), offering up comments that make you feel worse than before you said the affirmation, which is the opposite of its purpose!

Don't judge believability by what you know can happen for you, but by what has a sliver of truth and possibility. Even just a little bit of truth goes a long way.

For example, saying "I am a millionaire," when you're clearly not, is going to create a lot of pushback. But saying "I *think* like a millionaire" is more believable if you've researched the mindset of a millionaire and started employing that type of thinking.

Create that "feel good" factor!

Lastly, powerful affirmations make you feel good. This is not the time to use fancy words (unless they energize you!), weak words, tongue-tying words, or complicated sentences. Make your affirmations simple, meaningful to *you*, and juicy.

This is where you could have one or two affirmations that technically use negative wording but create an overwhelmingly positive effect. For example: "I am limitless! I am unstoppable!" If your affirmation makes you feel like you have superpowers, it can't be wrong.

One that I use as more of an alert statement is: "Drop the drama." In three little words, it snaps me out of those moments when I'm entertaining stories of what might have happened, what I "know" someone's thinking about me, or hypothesizing some dreadful event sure to come. It's my positivity stun gun!

Examples of powerful affirmations

Relationships:

I AM getting better each day at communicating clearly and honestly.

I AM seeing the love in _____'s interactions with me.

I AM growing deeper, more loving relationships every day.

My relationships are respectful, soul-filling, and joyful.

I AM love.

It is safe and pleasurable to give and receive love.

I AM seeing each day as a chance to serve others through compassion and kindness.

I AM choosing to spend my time with people who elevate me.

My relationships are nourishing to my heart and soul.

I AM seeing the best in others.

Career:

Every day is play with purpose.

I AM making a difference in my own way.

I AM able to see the good in what I do.

I AM a valuable member of my company/ organization.

In every challenge, there's an opportunity.

Finances:

My needs are met ahead of time, before I even know to ask for them.

I AM making the best choices for my financial future.

I AM effortlessly attracting financial abundance.

I AM a money magnet!

Money flows easily to me because I think positive thoughts about money.

Money is a cool tool I use to spread joy and fun in my life.

I AM attracting the income I desire.

I AM blessing what I want.

Self:

"I surrender to what is. I let go of what was. I have faith in what will be." –Sonia Ricotti

I AM creating the life I want.

I have a purpose. I AM essential to Life.

I AM creating my own perfect possibilities. If something better exists, it's there for me to discover.

I AM enough. I AM worth it.

Every choice I make is loving and supportive to myself.

I AM taking care of myself in the best possible ways so I can take care of others.

The answers I seek are always within me.

I deserve the best life has to offer.

I AM open to receiving miracles daily.

I choose to be brave. I AM brave.

I AM beautiful, inside and out.

I only think and do things that are kind and loving to myself.

I support my body in being its healthiest, most vibrant form, whatever that may be.

Exercise 12: Create Affirmative Affirmations (Time: 5 minutes)

Construct at least one affirmation you could use for each Life Area to support you right now—Relationships, Career, Finances, Self. You can use one of the examples above, but make sure it speaks to you, so edit as necessary.

Beneath that, construct a few affirmations that lead you to your Future Self and your Big Dream Life. Write those down too.

Position your affirmations where you'll see them often. You could write each affirmation on a piece of paper, notecard, or Post-it note and stick them on your wall, mirror, in your car, bag, locker, wallet, anywhere you will see it throughout the day. You could set your phone to send your affirmations as reminders, or take a picture of a written affirmation and set it as your home screen. Put them in your way.

Affirmations do have their limits. Even if you have the most potent affirmations known to humankind, they won't guarantee success. Even if you say them repeatedly, and actually believe them, it doesn't mean they'll come to pass.

Affirmations are a tool, like a hammer in a toolbox. If your desired end result is a lovely home, simply having a world-class hammer doesn't mean anything will get built. The hammer has to be used—action has to be taken over a period of time—in conjunction with other specific tools, in order for any structure to materialize. But having the appropriate, quality tools and using them consistently will get you much closer to your dream home than not using the tools—or not having them in the first place.

There's another tool you can use, which turns the words and concepts of affirmations into visual representations, making them come alive for you. This tool is a ...

Vision Board

You might have heard about vision boards before. It's a surface, either physical or virtual, that contains a collection of images representative of what you're looking to have show up in your life.

Vision boards are another commonly talked about self-help tool that's similarly misunderstood and underutilized. Perhaps you've created one before and it sat unused and unappreciated (I was in this category).

It's not about sticking a bunch of pictures up and calling it a day. Nothing will come out of that, except perhaps a nice collage. Instead, this process should be intentional and deserves to be taken seriously.

The good news is that, by now in this book, you're way ahead of someone approaching a vision board cold. Your vision board will very quickly hold significance to you because you've already done all the preparation work that'll make the board meaningful.

But what about all those lists I had you create, along with your Big Dream Life Declaration (Chapter 5, Exercise 10), and your Future Self discovery (Chapter 6, Exercise 11)? You might be thinking: *Those provide all the details of my Big Dream Life! Aren't those enough?*

Those lists and vivid details were crucial in creating your vision of your future, and are still valuable to reference. But what often happens to those writings is they remain in your notebook or on your computer, and are only read when you remember, if ever again. You do have the advantage of having done the work, so it's with you, but it's easily forgotten in our busy lives. Wouldn't it be more effective to, in a matter of seconds, be able to conjure up your Big Dream Life just from seeing some images?

I recommend finding your pictures online, either through a search engine, free image database, or visual community such as Pinterest. It's so much easier and more efficient than going through magazines or printed materials. To create a physical board, you could print each photo out and add it to a poster board, or create a collage on your computer and then print out a copy.

Your visual representations can be literal if you like that. If you want to attract your soul mate, and know what qualities you seek in that person or relationship, you could find a photo of a couple holding hands or laughing, enjoying each other's company in some way. It doesn't mean you think you are or look like those people. They simply represent the feeling or quality you want in your romantic relationship.

You can also include images that hold symbolic meaning. For example, a feather can represent freedom or taking flight to seek a new perspective.

One way to take your vision board to another level is to mix in your affirmations and details of Your Heart's Desires list (Chapter 2, Exercise 3) with your images. I did this in a PowerPoint presentation, using one to two slides for each Life Area and subcategory. The benefits are having everything in one place and the inclusion of details to my visual cues. The best part is I can play it like an inspirational mini movie before bedtime to send me off into great dreams, or in the morning to start my day on a positive note.

However, your vision board doesn't have to be your complete life and everything you want to accomplish and do in order to gain benefits—that may be too broad and unwieldy of a way to look at it.

Here are two focused ways to approach your vision board:

1. Take one specific area you want to focus on and go really deep with it. For example, if you want to have stronger connections with the people in your life, you might want to only address relationships (spouse, kids, friends, family, co-workers, neighborhood, etc.). Take some of your goals with that, affirmation-related, and find images that remind you of the Dream Life that involves the relationships in your life. So you have the pictures, but also affirmations and goals.

2. Take a couple aspects of your life where you desire change and explore those. Let's say you want to find your soul mate and be financially free. You add goals and affirmations and find images that have to do with that.

The purpose of your vision board is to spark your memory of your Big Dream Life. Then you take a few minutes in the morning (or some other time during the day) and dive into that aspect. For approach #2, you might look at your financial area and ask: What would my life look like if I was financially free? Enjoy where your imagination takes you and pay close attention to how you feel in that moment. You might get an idea for an action step you can take.

One note of caution: There's no point in showing your board to anyone. It's not going to mean the same thing to them. Even though it's exciting to you and therefore you might want to share it, other people aren't going to grasp what it's about and what you're doing with it. (I will be speaking in more detail in Chapter 10 about the pitfalls of sharing your dreams too early.)

Now, let's get started ...

Exercise 13: Your Vision Board (Time: 1–2 hours)

I recommend doing your vision board in one session, or by scheduling time over a few days specifically for this activity. But begin as soon as possible—how about right now? Otherwise, before you know it, a week or a month has gone by and you haven't finished it.

Don't try to make your board so perfect that you don't get it done. You want it to be visually pleasing, but it's not going to hang in an art gallery. You can keep adding to your board later. It will always be a work in progress, and that's good!

Block off the time for this exercise. Schedule it! Don't get lost in the Internet rabbit hole if you venture online. Close out your Facebook and email, and turn off your notifications. Consider this exercise your job when you're doing it. This is going to play a major role in helping you to visualize what you want (and therefore manifest it), so make it a priority.

The Magic of Visualization

Visualization is not magic in and of itself. The magic comes from how you *use* visualization. Repeatedly envisioning your desired outcome gets you accustomed to the idea and primes your mind to believe in its possibility.

The process of repeated visualization, research, practice, and trying things on actually protects you from the consequences of your desires. What do I mean? Say your goal is to have a lot of money. Going from pauper to kingly status is a big change. If you're not prepared, the shift would be unsettling and possibly harmful to you, as new and plentiful responsibilities and expectations are dumped into your lap. But if you've spent a lot of time visualizing your wealth, addressing all the unsupportive thoughts that spring forth, and stepping into the mindset of a wealthy person ... it won't be such a shock.

If part of your Big Dream requires you to be a really great public speaker, it could be daunting to imagine jumping into if it's far from what you're comfortable with or may have ever done outside of a school presentation.

Start envisioning a scenario that pushes you past your comfort zone. If it's scary enough to imagine speaking in front of a few people, start with that. You don't even have to know what your material would be. The scene could be silent, with you in front of the room, smiling, engaging your audience, receiving positive feedback, and getting your point across. Feel what it would feel like to have successfully presented your speech and bask in the glory.

When that's comfortable, you can proceed to imagine yourself addressing a larger audience with a microphone, such as a town hall, auditorium, or theater. Then perhaps you imagine speaking to an arena of people, complete with those big screens that broadcast your delivery.

This is just an example of how visualization could strengthen and prepare you for your dream. Certainly, speaking in public is not for everyone. Apply this example to your own dream, and begin visualizing.

Priming yourself for your dreams doesn't happen through visualization alone. There are action steps you can take to bring your visions to life.

Find an example.

Seek out examples of the kind of energy you want to portray. Using the example of public speaking again, you could analyze how role model presenters command the stage and the room. Watch a lot of speeches. Look at how they've constructed their material (using stories, jokes, facts/research, personal anecdotes). TED talks are usually a great resource because the people who get invited to speak have quite a bit of experience under their belts *[TED is a nonprofit that hosts short talks on ideas in Technology, Entertainment, and Design]*.

Practice.

As they say, practice makes perfect. Imagining without practice isn't going to seal the deal. You won't become a world-class speaker if you've never done it. And you won't be starting in the big leagues, even if your visualizations have gotten you there already.

There are usually ways you can put your goals and visualizations into action, even if it's on a small scale. Returning to public speaking again: even if you didn't start making public speeches, you can work on implementing tips and skills into your everyday conversations. Think of yourself already as a public speaker. Whenever you can, even if it's small talk, start implementing what you've learned (like eye contact) and imitate your favorite speakers.

You can start practicing elements of your Dream Life today—and you should! You'll be aligning with your wants, your visualizations, vision board, and solidifying your dreams. If you start to get nervous or unsure, recite your affirmations, such as "I AM a successful, magnetic, entertaining public speaker. Public speaking comes effortlessly, and joyfully to me, and I love it!"

Your affirmations are not just there to say for the heck of it. You're using them while you experience things, learn, and take action. It becomes a part of you—a belief as sure as your knowing that the Earth is round. That's when things come alive and start working for you.

Try it on.

If part of your dream involves a different lifestyle, put yourself in that environment as much as possible. You could visit furniture showrooms and look for things you're going to have or spend time sitting on a spectacular couch, imagining this will be yours. If you know the kind of clothes your Future Self will wear, go to a clothing store that has your style and try clothes on. Have a car in mind? Go take it for a test drive. Window shop for real estate online, zeroing in on your favorites and imagining yourself living there. Or, better yet, go to an open house. Let me stress that you're not buying anything—you're visualizing. And also important to note is that you will need to catch any negative thinking. Banish any chatter along the lines of "I can't afford this," which will direct your focus on how far this aspect is from your current reality. Instead, think something like:

This is mine.
This is part of my everyday life.
This is meant for me.
This is SO ME!

These try-ons aren't a waste of time. You are doing everything you can to bring your Dream Life *to life*!

Affirmations and visualizations are important tools in preparing you for all the blessings and gifts coming your way, which gets you used to this "new" life safely and with positive anticipation. Soon, it will start to feel normal—you'll expect these great things to happen. Since your outside world is a reflection of your inside world, seeing what you want and feeling good about it will facilitate that life coming true and send you right into your Big Dream Life.

8

MAP THE DREAM

Nothing is particularly hard if you divide it into small jobs.

–HENRY FORD

Your dream is probably far away, or seems far away, right? You may be wondering how the heck you're supposed to get there. We're going to map out the exact steps you will take, so that you can see an actionable path to your dreams.

For most of my life, I didn't have issues visualizing my dreams and identifying some embedded goals, but I wasn't successful in outlining the details. So I was left with some Big Dreams and nothing to lead me out of feeling overwhelmed as I stared at the expansive distance between where I stood and my intended destination.

That's why I included the following Big Dream Breakdown exercise. It breaks your impressively big goals down into manageable tasks or focus points so you can actually achieve them. You know the saying, "How do you eat an elephant?" Bite by bite, step by step, you'll begin to live the life you imagined.

Writing these things down doesn't mean you'll achieve them, or it'll happen in the timeframe you plan. However, writing them down:

- Reinforces your commitment to them.
- Promotes higher retention and recall.
- Provides accountability.
- Focuses you on your direction and goals.

If this is your first time doing this kind of exercise, it might be a little confusing. I have included an example portion from my own past Big Dream Breakdown after the exercise directions. Your breakdown will be much more involved and all-encompassing, but for simplicity, I have chosen one component of my Career Life Area, as well as a Bucket List item and creative goal as the focus so you can see how the breakdown might look.

[*Want a printable blank version of the Big Dream Breakdown? If you haven't already, visit www.KristinRath.com/meant-for-more-bonus-materials to download the worksheet, along with additional bonus materials that go along with this book.*]

Exercise 14: Big Dream Breakdown (Time: 40 minutes–1 hour)

At the top of a sheet of paper, write *5 Years*, followed by the month, day, and year exactly five years from today.

Down the next several pages, space out the labels *3 Years*, *1 Year*, *6 Months*, *3 Months*, *1 Month*, *3 Weeks*, *2 Weeks*, *1 Week*, *Tomorrow*, *Today*. Make sure you write down the date for each. Doing so takes these durations from abstract to concrete.

You're going to be spending a good amount of time on this. Don't skimp on this step. If you aren't able to commit this amount of time in one sitting, do this exercise for each Life Area separately (perhaps over a few sessions), which will focus you and not require as much time as it would to plan out your whole Big Dream Life.

In Five Years

Think of what you'll need to be, know, and have done at this point to be on course for your Big Dream Life.

Where will you be in your journey? What qualities will your life have? If you know a location you'll be, what you'll be doing, how you'll show up in the world—write it all down.

If you get stuck, or find the big picture overwhelming, start with the area of your life you most want to see changes in or requires the most change. You may want to continue on with just this aspect until you zero in on today's actions, then do the same process with other elements of your life in the Big Dream (like the recommendation for those with less time). I found that starting on the Life Area I wanted to experience the most change in (Career) got me going, and then sparked other related Life Area plans (Self, Financial, Relationship) as my goals took shape.

Later on, you might want to list the timeline for each Life Area separately, if that makes more sense to you. This is particularly important if working toward goals in all four Life Areas will be overwhelming.

If you have something planned that takes a specific amount of time (higher education, training, certifications, etc.) make sure you add a realistic timeframe for this and fill in as many details as possible about how you see your life.

In Three Years

Based on everything you've written down for what life will be like five years from now, ask yourself the same questions. What will you be an expert at, need to know, and still have to learn to reach the life you see in five years? The same guidelines outlined above apply.

In One Year

Now it becomes easier to plan more specifically. What do you need to have accomplished in a year to be on track for your three-year vision? This should be much more specific than the three-year or five-year mark.

In Six Months

What are a couple goals you want to achieve by this point to accomplish your larger goals and live the life you imagine one year from now? Give each of these goals specific dates—When will you start? When will you finish?—and other details.

In Three Months

What will you have accomplished by this time to support your six-month goals?

In One Month

What actions can you have taken by this time to set you up for success in Month 3?

In Three Weeks

By this time, I suggest pulling out a calendar or daily planner. Now you'll break down what you'll have accomplished or see in a month into small, actionable steps. You might want to take what you discover here, and further down the countdown, and divvy them up for each day or designate what days and hours you can schedule this work. This is where it gets really exciting because you'll start seeing the little steps you can take toward the change you want to see!

In Two Weeks

As your goals get distilled closer to today, it gets really real. You might be doubting your ability to get your steps done. It's okay. Feel the fear and do it anyway—write it down and remind yourself why you're doing all this!

In One Week

These will be even more specific. Challenge yourself to take massive action! Don't let the critics be louder than your Big Dream!

Tomorrow!

What is one thing you can do tomorrow to set into motion your Week 1 goals? There's always at least one action you can take ... like reading the next chapter of this book, which will address developing and adopting habits to support you on your journey!

Today!

What is one thing you can do today? Even a tiny step counts! Maybe spend a few minutes visualizing how awesome it will be to accomplish your Week 1 goals!

As you might recall, my answer for what I wanted if there was nothing holding me back was "heal the world." One way I see myself contributing to that end is sharing my experiences and knowledge of joyful living, self-love, and empowerment—you're holding one of my contributions in your hands right now!

Although there are multiple paths that can bring me to that result, my passion for connecting with others, my comfort in being onstage, and my love for travel combine into the idea of a career as an international motivational speaker. Furthermore, there are many steps that deal with expanding one's network and public reach that could lead up to worldwide speaking engagements.

Below is a sample portion of my Big Dream Breakdown exercise from August 2015, which I provide to show you how it can look. The focus is on my Career Life Area, but it includes some goals from my Self Life Area that have to do with travel and creative hobbies:

5 Years August 18, 2020

Career Life Area: Book first speaking engagement as Keynote Speaker, with 500+ in attendance. Third book becomes international best-seller. Podcast is now a documentary series that features interviews with thought leaders in Personal Transformation.

Self Life Area: Crossed off five travel destinations from Bucket List.

3 Years August 18, 2018
Career: Second best-selling book published, with national tour. Podcast is #1 in category on iTunes.
Self: Crossed off two destinations from Bucket List.

2 Years August 18, 2017
Career: Online course based on book launches. Start preparing for podcast launch (January 2018). Two self-help articles have been published in major online/print outlets.

1 Year August 18, 2016
Career: First self-help book written, with publication date by end of year.
Self: Visited one of my travel goals.

6 Months February 18, 2016
Career: Compile list of topics to write articles for blog and article submissions.
Self: Get a friend to commit to joining me on first Bucket List adventure!

3 Months November 1, 2015
Career: Submit admissions packet.

1 Month September 16, 2015
Career: Take grad school entrance exam. Secure references for application.

3 Weeks September 8, 2015
Self: Start savings account for Bucket List travel. Create alerts for air travel to those destinations.

2 Weeks September 1, 2015
Self: Perform in poetry reading. Commit to one event per month (attendance or performance).

1 Week August 25, 2015
Career: Research all important dates and deadlines for grad school.
Self: Write new poem for poetry reading.

Tomorrow August 19, 2015
Career: Schedule grad school entrance exam and go over materials.

Today August 18, 2015
Self: Compile my must-visit travel destinations from Bucket List.

[I didn't detail it here for the Bucket List travel, but if you have goals that require financial planning, write those steps in as well (amount of money to save, by when, and how). Also, if there are important dates that fall in-between what I have here, or you want to include, schedule those in as well. For example, I mapped out each tiny step I had to take for my graduate school application process, with official or self-appointed due dates.]

In my example, there were some factors that threw off timing, altered my course, and created challenges that turned out to be blessings. I had originally anticipated starting graduate school in the spring of 2016 (granting acceptance into the program) but soon after starting the application process, I was told the school had discontinued their spring semester start. This significantly moved my timeline (bump in the road), with a start date the following fall. Additionally, I decided to take the entrance exam one more time because I wasn't happy with my initial score (small setback).

The gift was that I was contacted by the director of another program (that I didn't initially think I was qualified for) to let me know there was a more advanced program perhaps better suited for me (and it was!). This program, incidentally, didn't require the standardized test (Arrrgh! Unnecessary detour!). However, I decided to see the time and effort I spent on that test as preparation for the intense academic schedule that followed. When I wrote out my goals, I wasn't certain about my graduate school acceptance, nor the schedule of the program, so after that was defined, I decided to postpone my Bucket List travel until after graduation, and instead take smaller trips and day-excursions that were still on my "must-do" list.

Another important goal of mine was writing a book that would help others. At the time I declared this goal, I had no idea what it would be about. But I didn't dismiss it. I allowed my thoughts to circle around the book until it would start to create stress—*What am I going to write about? How is this going to happen?*—and then let the idea go, reminding myself that the topic would come to me when the timing was right. Then, in June of 2016, I decided to brainstorm on paper all the possible book topics I could write ... and that was the day this book was born.

Some of my goals changed entirely, such as substituting continued poetry readings and performances with West African drumming classes. I wasn't so concerned with *how* I experienced creativity, but rather that I satisfied my creative needs on a consistent basis.

We do the things we have to do first—especially the things that make us money—and put the "unnecessary" stuff off. Days, weeks, years, maybe a whole lifetime can go by and we never did those things on our "One of These Days" list, even though they were important to us. Those are called *regrets*. Regrets are the last thing you want to be left with at the end of your life.

Make sure you schedule the items from your wish list, Bucket List, and goals sheet. The more specific you are, the more likely you'll follow through because you're clear on what the goal is. For example, if you want to read more, specify what "more" is, such as "I read two books a month." Start bringing your wish lists to life by taking action on them *now*.

You should refer back to the Big Dream Breakdown document often. As the goals you've set for a year from now come closer, you'll want to rewrite your breakdown, adding in those weekly/monthly steps while imagining additional goals for the future.

Keep in mind, much of your plan may not turn out as you laid it out, or in the timeframe you designated for it. Mine went off the rails (although with happy results) almost immediately! The goal isn't to follow your Big Dream Breakdown exactly as you've written it, ticking off each step along the way. The goal of this exercise is to be *continuously purposeful with your passions.* The Big Dream Breakdown is a living document—it should change with you as you evolve on your journey. Flow with the change, rather than resisting it, or else you'll miss the "something better."

So why write down these things at all, since you can't predict exactly how you'll get to your destination? Because in writing down a plan, you are putting things into motion. If you keep shooting for what you love to do, then it can't turn out wrong. Get into the habit of going for what you want. Figure out what makes you happy and fulfilled and then *do those things!*

Hopefully, you're less overwhelmed by the enormity of what your Big Dream Life holds. Now that you have charted your course, how do you make sure you follow it?

The next chapter will cover the importance of developing habits that support your road ahead, and what makes a successful routine.

9

DEVELOPING DREAM-HAPPY HABITS

We become what we repeatedly do.

-SEAN COVEY

You've done tremendous work! Now you have a map to your treasure in hand, and you see exactly how to get to that X that marks the spot. You can point out some concrete goal posts. You have a clear vision of where you're going and can experience it viscerally through visualizing and embodying your Future Self.

But even with all your significant progress, it takes more to make a lasting change in your life toward your dreams. You must develop the habits that'll support you and consistently implement what you've learned until it becomes a part of you.

Here are some habits to install your internal GPS:

Habit #1: Start your day intentionally with a morning ritual.

This kind of ritual is not about superstition or tradition. It's about creating a routine—setting up your environment properly to get your mind and body primed for a productive, high-vibe day.

Think of a day when you held a clear idea of what you wanted to accomplish. That focus guided you as your day unfolded. It was easier to plan, because you chose activities that helped your goal, or at least didn't interfere with it. You probably achieved your intention too, and felt a sense of fulfillment from it.

Imagine that happening every day!

If the beginning of your day is usually a whirlwind, just five to ten minutes of intention-setting can make a huge difference. This can be done during your shower, while drinking your wake-up beverage, or on your commute. Set your intentions as soon after you get up as possible. It grounds you in positivity from the get-go.

Simple 4-Step Daily Ritual

1. **Look at your vision board and dive into your Big Dream Life.** Use your vision board to recall aspects of your Big Dream. Take one particular desire and immerse yourself in what it would feel like for you to achieve that and how it could come to be. Take a couple minutes to allow it to feel real. If in your Big Dream Life you focus on loving yourself unconditionally and being your

biggest supporter, what would that look and feel like?

2. **Set your intention for the day.** It's kind of like setting the day's soundtrack so you can move to its rhythm. Your intention could be something unrelated to what you've just visualized but something you'd like to bring more of into your life. For example: "I will treat myself with love today."

3. **Come up with 2–3 actions you can take to honor your intention.** Bringing more self-love into your day could mean carving out some time to start reading that book you're excited about. Or scheduling a massage. Or keeping your phone on silent and unchecked as you take a ten-minute walk. Or adding more nutritious snacks to your kitchen. Anything that is caring and loving to yourself would count, and it doesn't have to be complicated or take much time.

4. **Select an affirmation you could use throughout the day.** This is either directly related to your intention or something you feel will lift your spirits and keep your vibe high. For example: "I AM love."

While everyone is struggling to wake up and rev up, you're already energized. While others are weeding through their personal to-do lists, your day's goal is defined and actionable.

While others need cups of coffee and sugar to keep their energy going, you have a high-vibe affirmation to keep you perked and positive. Even if your plan doesn't go as intended, you at least *have* a plan and are headed in a positive direction. Your internal GPS is set, you're ready to go, and you are tuned in to opportunities.

I'd say waking up ten minutes early for that kind of result is worth it … wouldn't you?

Habit #2: Have a go-to mood booster kit.

Consider adding the following to your daily ritual or at regular intervals in your week, to keep centered and balanced—and, therefore, happier! These are just a handful of ideas. Add what works for you.

1. Meditation

In addition to numerous health benefits, meditation quiets the mind and soothes frazzled nerves. Focusing inward allows for inspiration to arise and for you to feel one with your surroundings, which can put those "small problems" into perspective. There are many kinds of meditation, but it doesn't have to be advanced or lengthy to provide results.

Simply focusing on your inward and outward breath can provide stress relief and a recharge. You can also try imagining a blank white screen in your mind and allow thoughts to come and go, with no attempt to pursue, explore, reject, or resist them.

2. Journaling

Journaling is used to record your thoughts and work things out. Sometimes just getting what's on your mind down on paper releases the burden or confusion of them. Then you can move on, instead of unnecessarily keeping them swirling through your head.

Rereading past entries can be helpful in seeing any transformations or shifts that have occurred, where you let go of an unsupportive belief, made a significant step, or adopted a perspective that wiped out what you previously considered a "problem." Journaling is a record of your own history. You're writing down moments that had an impact. The journey to the dream is your life, and it's a sacred story.

3. Gratitude Practice

A gratitude practice is simply focusing on that which you're thankful for. I do this several ways. At night, I might reflect on my day and what gifts arose and write them in my journal. This is a comforting nightcap that prepares me for a restful sleep. During the day, I take a minute to recognize all the things, people, and events I'm thankful for. Instantly, there's a smile on my face, my heart feels full, and my perspective is brighter.

It's easiest to look at what's right in front of you and give appreciation. Even on your most difficult day, you probably have food, shelter, clothes, and clean water, right?

One of the things that really brings out gratitude in me is nature. I go so far as to lay my hands on the trunk of a tree, hold rocks, or stand on the grass in my bare feet. Nature is such a powerful ally in being in the moment and giving thanks. I can thank a tree for the oxygen it gives me, providing a habitat for living things, delivering beauty, and shading me from the sun. I also try to express gratitude "for no reason" to friends and family. I never want to have that moment of *I wish I'd told them how much they mean to me.*

There is so much to be grateful for, if you look for it. And with that focus, you immediately turn up your vibration to joy, peace, and love. From these states, you're able to reset and move forward.

Habit #3: Schedule what's important.

As I've mentioned before, if it's important to you—schedule it. If it's part of your Big Dream Breakdown, it's even more crucial to chart those steps. If we wait to see if we have time to tick off our action steps, our days get filled up and they usually won't get done. Treat your plan for your dreams with as much respect and dedication as you would a paid job.

Habit #4: Nourish your mind and body.

Nourishment can come from learning. Whether or not you were a "good student" before, you have been a student of your life throughout this book. You've studied your own life through these chapters and done your homework through their exercises. Keep that curiosity and thirst for knowledge. You never know everything. In fact, the more you know, the more you realize how much you *don't* know. Learning keeps life exciting and will support you as you travel on your dream path.

This book gives you the framework for your dreams. It's not all you need, however. Life is rich and multi-layered. There's more to add to your toolkit and journey than I can imagine for you. It's up to *you* to discover what will support you, propel you forward, and become part of your life. I have included resources at the end of this book that were part of my own journey. Maybe they'll be part of yours, too, or maybe not. Do your own exploration. Your journey is a deeply personal experience that will look like no one else's. It won't be wasted time to find out what works for you.

Naturally, nourishment is also about taking care of your health. Be aware of what you put into your body. Food affects energy, mood, brain activity, joint flexibility, and muscle quality. Pure water is needed to flush out toxins, both physical and mental, and facilitate optimal function on all levels. Our bodies were meant to move, and since modern life involves quite a bit of sitting, make an effort to add mindful movement into your daily life. I'm not talking about exercise programs and regimes (that's for you and your doctor to decide). What I mean is making time to move your body in a way that feels good and makes sense for you. Your health is an extension of your mind. They support each other.

Treating your mind and body with respect and love allows your total self to be at its best.

Habit #5: Find your tribe.

Surround yourself with people who are like-minded, inspirational, and who do things you want to do. As motivational speaker, author, and entrepreneur Jim Rohn said, "You are the average of the five people you spend the most time with."

It's not always possible to only be around positive, supportive people, so make sure there are a lot of others who do fit the energy and direction you seek for yourself. Connecting with those whom you admire is a way to start being those qualities they share with your Future Self.

Find some people who are more successful than you. They'll root you on, spark ideas, and inspire you to rise to the occasion. These people will be generous with their advice and knowledge, and treat themselves and others well. While it's possible to meet members of your tribe in your daily life, it's also possible—and more practical—to seek them out. Research groups and organizations that interest you. Use the power of the Internet and find them.

There are also people who can serve as mentors. They can guide and help you, and provide advice, information, and perspective on your journey. Identify people you can emulate or learn from. A good role model is someone who is successful in a way that's meaningful to you. They aren't magic—they didn't wake up that way—they worked at it. They had experiences and figured out their own processes. Find out what they do, think, and know that contributes to their success. What are their morning rituals, what energizes them and keeps them on a successful path? Who are *their* mentors?

Those who are most in line with their passion have particular habits and routines they rely on. These differ from person to person, but they share consistency and discipline in common.

***

There are so many choices today and so much information thrown at us, that it can be easy to go from one fad to another or not try something out that may support us. That's why it is important to develop a routine and mood-boosting kit based on your own self-study.

The next section will provide additional support for you on your journey: how to deal with people, reconciling with a non-dream job, and how to pick up and dust off after setbacks.

SECTION FOUR:
TRAVEL SUPPORT

10

DEALING WITH PEOPLE

When dealing with people, remember you are not dealing with creatures of logic, but with creatures of emotion ...

-DALE CARNEGIE

I hope your Big Dream Life is starting to feel possible.

You've been vividly imagining it, have mapped out possible steps, and maybe it's beginning to take hold within you. As much as possible, keep up your positive vibes and direction.

Even so, you may find that it's a challenge to stay in that energized and exciting world you've created while in the "real world." We don't live in a bubble—we do have to deal with people, many of whom don't have the knowledge you now have and aren't on the same wave length. You may have even encountered some of these challenges since you started this course. Negativity, limited thinking, unsupportive comments, and unloving actions from others can take a toll.

How do you deal with the outside world messing with your flow? By choosing how you interact with others and by choosing how you perceive your experience.

Here are some points to keep in mind:

Protect your Big Dream and goals.

Sharing your goals with a trusted, supportive person is a great way to provide accountability. When you tell that person about what you're reaching for, there's going to be a follow-up conversation, which can help keep you on track.

But remember when I suggested not showing your vision board to anyone? Well ...

Be judicious as to what you share of your Big Dream with others, how much of it you reveal, and when you do it. Do a slow unveiling of your dream so it isn't unplugged before you've started with just a couple comments from someone else.

I've experienced this "bursting of the bubble" many times. I was psyched by my plans and wanted to share them. Then I did ... and instead of getting a mirror image of my excitement, I got silence—or, worse, lots of those "How?" questions. I ended up irritated or deflated, and if their fears mirrored mine, I perceived that as confirmation of my imminent failure. And just like that, I thought it was a stupid idea or the timing wasn't right and I should wait until I had the resources, knowledge, experience, etc.

If you have people who are dependent upon you and your dream affects them, it's a good idea to communicate your intents with them once they're fleshed out and se-cure. You'll have to deal with their fears, doubts, and worries, just as you had to overcome your own, so be prepared for that.

Listen to their feedback objectively. They may be able to uncover minefields you hadn't thought of before, which is a good thing, because you can either decide it's not something you need to deal with now (or ever!) or you can find the solution. Everything has a solution; it just needs to be discovered. It's also possible that your loved ones will be inspired by you, or perhaps they will help by providing encouragement and taking some re-sponsibilities and tasks off your plate.

If you've gotten this far in the book, you acknowledge that your Big Dream Life is important to you. Sometimes we put our dreams on hold or let go of them completely because we feel we should honor someone else's first. You need to understand that the Universe provides enough space in which to fit your dreams—as well as the resources to accommodate it—along with everyone else's.

Be careful not to take on other people's energy.

Have you ever been in a great place in your mind and then encountered people who are complaining about life and work and the state of the world, and by mid-morning you feel heaviness, irritation, or sadness for no reason? What's happened is you've taken on the energy of your environment.

If you suddenly have this uncomfortable energy and you don't know why, ask if it's even yours. Who have you been spending time with? What was the positivity level of the conversation or vibe they gave off?

(Remember Chapter 4: it could also be your own thoughts bringing you down. Thoughts create feelings, so take note of your mind chatter.)

Taking on energy or being affected by the energy around you doesn't make you an easily manipulated person. We're all affected by energy, whether we're aware of it or not. Everything is made up of energy—even us—and energy is easily transferable.

When you become more attuned to what's happening within you and outside you, you may pick up more of these feelings. When this happens, you can deal with them by applying the techniques you've learned to return to a higher state of mind—such as meditating, affirmations, reframing your perspective, stripping away the story (and therefore the emotional effect)—or choose one of your go-to mood boosters.

Be responsible for your own energy and how you show up.

As careful as you want to be with handling others' energy, you have to be as careful of what energy you put out and any role you play in contributing to it.

Communicate your wants and needs honestly and clearly.

If you've decided you want to implement a daily ritual or quiet time that will take place in the vicinity of other people, clearly communicate when it's happening and the importance of not being disturbed.

People aren't mind readers. Even if you've spent your whole life with someone—even if they seem to be able to read your thoughts or you think they *should*—they can't possibly know your every need. Especially if you're undergoing change—as you are with this book—your wants can be hard for another to predict.

Have you ever wanted to help someone but not known what to do? Didn't you wish they would just tell you what to do and you'd do it? Make your family's life easier, and you happier, by communicating your wants and needs when they involve loved ones. Don't make them guess—that only sets them up to fail.

Realize people have their own baggage.

When people lash out and dump on you, realize that it's not about you, even if they say it is. It comes from their perception and processing of a situation. Just as you have sabotaging, unsupportive, destructive thoughts—they do, too. Haven't you ever reacted unfairly to someone?

Dissolve all the story and emotion of an unpleasant interaction. Realize that their reaction isn't about you, and don't engage in the drama.

Have compassion.

You've become aware of your weaknesses, uncovered subversive thinking, and identified cross-purposes where your beliefs don't match up with your desires. You're also going to start being adept at spotting these things in other people.

However ...

Your awesome transformation doesn't give you license to judge or correct others. They have their own journey to take and the same rights for it to unfold in its unique way, just as you do.

***

There will be times others may take the wind out of your sails. Not everyone will cheer you on or agree with your choices. But that should not change you or your Big Dream. The goal is to boldly live the life you were meant to live—remaining steadfast despite any negativity from others—while respecting that everyone is free to walk their own path. It's a balancing act, but with the tools and knowledge you have now, you are empowered to choose your own experience.

11

DEALING WITH A NON-DREAM JOB

Either I will find a way, or I will make one.

–Phillip Sidney

We don't always have the job we want right now, nor the financial cushion to leave a job for one we do want or to pursue our dream full-time. So what can you do if you're in a less-than-ideal working situation?

Apply all of the things you've learned, including reframing your idea about the circumstance. Perhaps you've said: "I can't stand this job. I can't wait to get out of here!" Maybe now, instead, you can see it as an opportunity to experience it as something different.

When you do feel fulfilled, life's problems don't bother you as much. The good stuff going on in your life will sustain you. It creates an invisible armor around you. You can approach the job with more positivity, flexibility, and acceptance. That job you used to dislike will feel manageable. Nothing about the job will have changed, but you will have. Therefore, your perception of, and experience with, the job will change.

If you are in need of a job or would like to find a job you enjoy, the next two exercises will be useful in brainstorming possibilities.

The first step is to identify your strengths, which is the purpose of Exercise 15. That is immediately followed by Exercise 16, which explores how to monetize your strengths. Doing so can augment your non-dream job income or eventually grow into a dream job.

Exercise 15: Identify Your Strengths (Time: 5 minutes)

Write down your answers to the following questions:

What do you excel at?
- Skills you have
- Hobbies you enjoy
- Tasks you do easily
- What others come to you for when they need help, advice, or a job done

What favorable qualities or characteristics do you have?
- What you appreciate in yourself
- What others admire or appreciate in you
- What has helped you achieve goals

In what situations do you thrive? How do you work best?
- Needing silence and isolation vs. requiring a social and cooperative environment

Exercise 16: Monetize Your Superpowers (Time: 5 minutes)

Consider whether your strengths can be turned into a job that earns money.

People will pay for:

- What they don't want to do or don't have time to do themselves.
- What they don't know how to do or don't do well.
- What will provide them comfort or pleasure.
- What will ease their pain or fix their problem.

What do you love and would do for free, or already do for free? Could this be something that makes you money? Look at your strengths list from Exercise 15, and for each one, ask if it's something you could make money from. Does it fulfill a need for someone? Is it a service you can provide or a product you can sell? Any of these can lead to well-paid work.

I didn't consider writing as a way to earn a living until about six years ago. Although I've enjoyed writing since I learned how to form letters, penned short stories and poems for fun, and wrote acclaimed essays in school, I never considered it something I could pursue as an avenue for income. It wasn't until I was so unhappy with my job as a waitress (during my actress-life stint) that I felt compelled, for the first time in many years, to write a poem expressing my feelings. I shared this writing with a loved one who firstly, didn't know about my writing ability, and secondly, asked me why I didn't do this for a living.

The question floored me. It hadn't crossed my mind in my adult life. A question posed from someone else opened up my eyes to this possibility and how it could pan out. I had absolutely no idea how to proceed—and I didn't yet have the knowledge I'm passing along to you in this book—but I felt I'd found the answer to a long-unfulfilled void. It was scarily exciting and I was determined not to linger in my thoughts, but to act on it.

My first action was to seek out guidance. I found a creative career coach, Melissa Rosati (the one who guided me through the visualization I shared in Chapter 6) who lovingly pushed me past my comfort zone and encouraged me to think beyond what I had ever imagined was possible.

With Melissa's suggestion, I started a blog on nutrition and well-being. I didn't know what it would lead to, but I enjoyed it. I became a student of holistic health, listened to people's conversations and pinpointed where there was a need for information, and created content that I hoped was practical and valuable. Pretty soon, I became known to my friends and co-workers as someone who knew about health and fitness. I started to build an online reputation as one too, through consistent effort and engagement—I'd identified my strength! Now for the monetization ...

My first job in the communications field resulted from a tweet. Through Twitter, a health company discovered my blog and hired me as a content writer for their website. I explored other ways to write and joined the International Women's Writing Guild—another recommendation of Melissa's. I began volunteering for them, which led to a part-time social media gig, and then evolved into a permanent part-time job with a range of responsibilities (a.k.a. opportunities for growth and acquiring new skills!). Based on recommendations, I received other work—such as teaching professionals social media, writing content for their sites, and proofreading their books for publication.

Things started happening for me once I opened my eyes to monetizing what I had once considered a hobby and then took massive action on it. I had no clue how it would all unfold, and I couldn't see my path clearly in the distance. But in time, each step revealed itself.

When you're enjoying something, you are in your sweet spot. You'll attract opportunities. Things will click from your alignment. If you don't see obvious ways to turn your skills and interests into employment, that's okay. But when you have these ideas percolating in your awareness, you can spot opportunities more easily.

The last chapter is also about dealing with less-than-ideal circumstances, but from a macro view. It's a reminder of some of the principles discussed throughout this book, with additional advice to support you on your Big Dream Life journey.

12

DEALING WITH POTHOLES, ROADBLOCKS, AND DETOURS

I may not have gone where I intended to go, but
I think I have ended up where I intended to be.

–DOUGLAS ADAMS

Even if you've planned your Big Dream Breakdown to a T, that doesn't guarantee that it'll turn out that way. How do you deal with setbacks, obstacles, and failures?

First of all, it's normal to feel lousy when they happen. But remember that the sensation will eventually pass. In the meantime, you can help yourself by creating and focusing on better thoughts, practicing self-care, and taking action that's supportive and loving—techniques you've learned in this book.

Secondly, setbacks aren't things you deal with once. They happen again and again throughout life. And when they happen, it's easy to get caught up in our thoughts, ruminate on the past and future, and get ourselves in trouble. We're human! The trick is to recognize the situation, be gentle with yourself, and take actions that bring you back into the moment so that you can re-center and restart.

Some loving reminders for you as you set out on your journey:

Allow for surprises and alternate paths.

While you may have a detailed vision of your Big Dream Life, resist setting your path in stone. Life is a dynamic, richly layered journey. You are a living, breathing, constantly changing being. Therefore, resist rigidity, which is the dark side of planning. Having your course mapped out gives you the flexibility and confidence to make adjustments.

Sometimes we want to rush to the destination. We're so excited to get there, we're practically salivating. After all the phenomenal work you've done here, you probably see your next steps right in front of you. It can be very frustrating when things don't pan out the way you planned, or aren't happening as quickly as you want them to.

Now that you've done all this planning, it's time to let it unfold as it will. You've dreamed and created; you believe in your creation and have faith in yourself and what the Universe can provide for you; you've calculated your steps and strategized what you can do. There is still the unfolding that has to happen. This will happen in its own time, not yours.

There's a proverb that says, "The best-laid plans of mice and men often go awry." It's true, but what causes us pain is our resistance to our plans changing. When we try to control our plans, and they go other than expected, that's when we experience pain. If we can allow for the possibility that we weren't able to dream up the best possible scenario on our first try—as humans with a limited capacity to know what's possible—or that what we're moving toward has an alternative path, then we alleviate that discomfort.

Don't be so narrowly focused on your dreams that you don't see the encompassing picture of life in general.

I struggle with this often. I see what I want and want to get there now! Especially when things start shifting and the awesomeness you've asked for (and taken action on) starts showing up. It's natural to want more of that—it's exciting! But it's also going to happen in the timeframe that it's supposed to happen. If you don't loosen your grip on what you expect and allow yourself to be in the moment, you're going to end up missing the little things in life. You'll experience more frustration, fear, anxiety, anger, and confusion.

Maybe it's not supposed to happen in this very moment. Go take a walk, play with your kids, talk to a friend, watch the sunset. Be in the moment. When I surrender and let that death grip go, I shift from being in my head to being back in my heart.

More times than not, in being present and seeing the beauty in life, I come to the revelations I have been seeking. When you're present and aware, you're hooking into your own intuition, allowing divine intervention to happen.

Practice self-love and care.

Practicing self-love and care includes things you enjoy and that make you feel good. Resist slipping into old, unsupportive habits. You're worth the effort. Revisit not only what your dream is, but why you're doing it. Your body is the vehicle that puts your soul's desires into action. Treat it well. You may need more rest while you process your discoveries and plans.

Your thoughts have potent power.

It's not the situation you're in, it's your thoughts *about* the situation you're in. Your thoughts dictate your mood, emotions, and experience. Your inside world shapes your outside world—you'll find that which will match your expectations, beliefs, and thinking. Your thoughts dictate how you feel about and perceive your journey. Happy thoughts equal happy feelings. Thoughts filled with fear, doubt, and shame make you feel anxious or paralyzed. Angry thoughts make you angry. If you're feeling a way you don't like, examine your thoughts. You have the choice to upgrade your feelings through upgraded thoughts.

Be aware that it's common to have old beliefs rise up from the trash heap as you encounter new situations, achievements, and your dreams become more "real." This doesn't mean you failed in some way. Your brain is just trying to do its job and protect you. Lovingly tell it that while you appreciate its intentions, you are the boss and will take it from here.

Get into a positive frame of mind before taking action.

To make better choices, it's essential to have better thoughts. Take the time to check in with where your head is at before taking any action toward your dreams. You want to be making decisions as your Future Self. Trying to tackle those to-do lists or creating and carrying out action plans while in a place of fear, doubt, and anxiety will impede or even completely stop your progress and results.

If you're feeling like you're in a less than desirable headspace, take the time to reframe with your go-to mood boosting techniques until your heart is open and your vibration is high. When you take action from *this* place, that's when incredible things happen!

Awareness and consistency is key.

You can't expect lasting change in your life by implementing what you've learned only one time, or maybe a couple times, or for only one thing. It's a daily practice that's as important as hydration. When you're dehydrated, you feel and perform poorly. When you take the time and effort and awareness to incorporate water throughout the day, you do well. After a while it becomes a natural part of your day, and if you were to stop drinking water, you'd feel the adverse effects even more acutely, and bring your awareness back to drinking more water again. You don't drink the optimum amount of water for one day and not worry about it ever again, do you? No. You have to keep doing it. Practicing the principles in this book is rather like that—instill it so deeply within you that it's as ingrained as your thirst for water.

Surrender to what can't be changed or controlled.

We only have control over ourselves—what we think, do, and experience. We don't have control over things or people outside of ourselves. If something happens beyond your control, do what you can (what is dependent upon *you*) and let go of the rest. If you find an obstacle, be flexible to think of another way. There's always a solution. You just have to find it.

Have unshakeable faith that Life is for you!

Faith has a wider scope beyond its connection to religion. It's about believing in Life and yourself so strongly that you don't need to always see proof.

You have faith in gravity, right? You know that when you jump up, you won't float up and away into space ... you'll come back down. Although gravity is an invisible force, we believe in it. Is it because we have such strong evidence of it that we believe, or does our belief in it dictate how much evidence we see?

You don't get to see all the miracles first and, because of them, have faith. Faith precedes the miracles. If this is challenging for you, examine your beliefs about faith, and use affirmations to remind yourself that you'll be okay no matter what. You can change your situation just by the way you look at it and take meaning from it. You have the power to find the way out.

Believing that life is teaming up with you to reach your dreams doesn't label you a Pollyanna-type character, wearing rose-colored lenses and living with your head in the clouds. Focusing on seeing what's good and right with life is you putting your intentions into practice— your life will be amazing, it's *already* amazing, and abundance and blessings are coming your way. You are open to receiving them and are attracting them through your work. It's only to your benefit to have faith in yourself and the Universe—what you put out into it, you will receive back.

Embrace obstacles, setbacks, and missteps as part of the journey.

In the depths of despair and frustration, when you're at the bottom—whatever that is for you—and you have nothing else to lose, you find yourself. You find out what really matters because everything else is stripped away. All the crap you thought mattered, doesn't. What's left are the essentials of what it means to be alive and what you want. But you don't need to hit bottom to figure it out. Use all those experiences of perceived failure, mistakes, and heartache to inform you. Use it because it taught you something. Even if the lesson was just to find out that a thing, person, or experience isn't for you.

Whether or not you believe that everything happens for a reason, isn't it better to see it that way? If you can reframe an obstacle, setback, or detour to see it as a chance to learn or grow or discover, it can get you through to the other side.

All those years I thought I'd wasted weren't wasted. They've come full circle to inform me, and provide the skills and experience I will need for these next steps in my Big Dream Life. You never know how missteps and side streets will play a role ... until the day you arrive at your destination.

Why not see the silver lining, the light at the end of the tunnel, and hold onto hope? Sometimes just a little bit of "magical thinking" can save you from being buried by hardships so you can get up and over it to see the other side.

***

Dare to dream big. Be brave. Practice being the best version of you. Plan and then let your journey unfold as it will. Take care of yourself. Have faith that miracles will follow. You have your feet firmly planted on your path. May your travels be better than you ever imagined.

MY SENDOFF TO YOU

Dear Fellow Travelers,

What a journey you've had!

- You've courageously and purposefully drawn out and spilled upon your pages the things others keep locked away from their own awareness and the possibility of change.
- You've looked through and dug up your questions and examined their origins and usefulness for your path ahead.
- You've created a safe space for yourself to imagine a world that fills your soul, loves you unconditionally, and mirrors the beauty inside you.
- You've recognized the power of your thoughts and the responsibility to use them with intention and care.
- You've stocked a recovery kit and know what to do in case of disaster and setback.

Congratulations! And thank you for trusting me to guide you. It was an honor.

Having completed this course, you are well on the way to your Big Dream Life.

Please cherish the wisdom of your heart and soul. Consult with them first before engaging your logical and interrogative mind. I want you to know that when you grow and transform, you'll bump into ceilings, scrape against walls, and struggle to push past barriers. Take this resistance as a sign you are at a fork in the road. You can stop and set up camp to avoid the discomfort, or journey on to reach the miracles waiting just around the bend, if you keep at it a little longer.

I believe in you. I believe in your dreams. Keep taking action. In bringing your dreams to light and life, you're making the world a better place for us all.

Wishing you joyous and fulfilling adventures,
Kristin

P.S. I would love honest feedback about your experience with *Meant for More.* Your opinion matters to me, and your review on Amazon helps others decide whether to read this book. www.amazon.com/author/kristinrath

ACKNOWLEDGMENTS

Bringing this book into the world took a village. I am so grateful for the support, encouragement, and guidance from my tribes: The International Women's Writing Guild, where I first found my voice as a writer; Strat Comm Cohort 5, a diverse, tightly knit group that challenges each other to be game-changing communicators; Self-Publishing School, for sharing its wealth of knowledge and community; my long-time cheerleaders, the Hot Mess Team; and my incredible family (the original tribe).

My mother's photography has awed me and others for decades, and I'm honored she contributed one of her images to the cover of this book. Thank you to artist Vraciu Andreea for her beautiful work in the cover design. A big thank you to my talented editor Spencer Hamilton, who wore many hats for me and provided an invaluable point of view.

But most of all, I thank my parents for their never-ending, unconditional love and belief in me. They inspire me to be the best I can be, every single day.

Photography, Jill Rath: www.facebook.com/jillrathauthor
Cover design, Vraciu Andreea: andreea3034@gmail.com
Editing, Spencer Hamilton: www.NerdyWordsmith.com

RESOURCES

This is a diverse group of people who share and teach information that spans topics from the metaphysical to the scientific. They were part of my journey to this moment. I have also included resources that have provided insight and inspiration to me. It might not all be for you, but there's certainly something in here that you may connect with and find value in.

Melissa Rosati - Creativity coach, branding specialist, and owner of Melissa's Coaching Studio, LLC. I'm grateful I listened to my inner guidance and decided to work with Melissa as a coach in 2009. My connection to her marked the beginning of my Big Dream Life path, so it's an honor to be able to call her a mentor and friend. http://www.melissarosati.com/

Jai Maa - Faith minister, seminar leader, motivational speaker, all-around goddess, and a personal friend. In her book, *Break Through Your Threshold: A Manual for Faith-Based Manifestation and Co-Creating With God*, she explains what a threshold is, the different kinds that can hold you back, and how to break through them to live your divine life. http://www.breakingthroughyourthreshold.com/

Riley Dayne - Following a near-death experience, this young man traveled the world in search for the answers to life's big questions. The result of his journey was *The Abundance Factor* movie, which includes interviews with

thought leaders in the realm of personal transformation. This incredibly valuable production encouraged my studies from some of the mentors I list here.
http://www.theabundancefactormovie.com/

Suzanna Kennedy – Author, speaker, Women's Empowerment Leader, Soul Purpose business coach. Suzanna teaches about energy, connection to Source, and how to reprogram your body and mind to express your true Divine Self. http://suzannakennedy.com/

Bruce Lipton – Stem cell biologist, author of *The Biology of Belief*, international speaker. His work demonstrates the power of our mind and the incredible choice we have in shaping our experiences.
https://www.brucelipton.com/

Dana Wilde – Brain trainer, speaker, host, author of *Train Your Brain*, CEO of The Mind Aware. Dana shows you how to harness the power of your mind to think positive thoughts that move you toward success. Her concentration is on business and leadership, but the principles can apply to everyone.
http://mindaware.danawilde.com/

Joe Vitale – Known as Mr. Fire, Joe is an energetic motivational speaker, marketer, and prolific author, including *Zero Limits: The Secret Hawaiian System for Wealth, Health, Peace, and More*. He shows you how to see problems as opportunities for solutions, and how to turn those ideas into products or services for business.
http://www.mrfire.com/

Sonia Ricotti – CEO/President of Lead Out Loud Inc. and the bestselling author of *Unsinkable: How to Bounce Back Quickly When Life Knocks You Down*. Dives deep into how our thoughts contribute to our unhappiness and how to rebuild your thoughts and stories into those that manifest a life even better than you can imagine. http://www.leadoutloud.ca/

Mindvalley Academy – A great resource for extraordinary living. They offer training in mind, body, spirit, and relationships. http://www.mindvalley.com/

Christie Marie Sheldon – Christie is a healer and intuitive who specializes in removing abundance blocks. From her, I learned the power of visualization, how to ask for what I want, to trust my intuition, and develop more connection to my psychic abilities (we all have them). Her bubbly personality creates a light, fun atmosphere in which to learn and explore. I came to her through Mindvalley Academy, but here is her personal website: http://christiesheldon.com/

T. Harv Eker – Dynamic motivational speaker, businessman, and author of the best-selling books, *Secrets of the Millionaire Mind* and *SpeedWealth*. Harv's focus is combining spirituality with wealth. His loud, nononsense, and sometimes shocking style isn't for everyone, but I learned some valuable financial perspective and business tips from him. http://www.harveker.com/

Oprah's SuperSoul TV – We all know who Oprah is, but perhaps not about the treasure trove of inspirational videos, films, and interviews she provides on her website. The SuperSoul Sessions are powerful TED-style talks by transformative influencers such as Iyanla Vanzant, Eckart Tolle, Deepak Chopra, Elizabeth Gilbert, Brené Brown, Shawn Achor, and Michael Bernard Beckwith. http://www.supersoul.tv/

Buddhism – I'm not Buddhist, but I have found value in aspects of this religion that are applicable to leading an enlightened, heightened life such as the practice of letting go, compassion, non-judgment, and mindfulness.

ABOUT THE AUTHOR

Professional tennis player, international businesswoman fluent in Japanese, Human Resources Manager, film and television actress...these were professions Kristin Rath pursued in an attempt to find her path. She committed to all of them, realizing only after years of pursuit that none was right for her. Sensing she was meant for more, Kristin set off on a decade-long journey of trial and error in search of her highest self's purpose. The framework of what she learned and discovered are in this book.

Kristin is currently following her calling, using her Master of Science degree in Strategic Communication from Columbia University (2017) to build a business centered around guiding others to lead their most joyful, authentic, and empowered lives.

To find out more about what Kristin is offering to help others live their Big Dream Life, visit www.KristinRath.com.

Printed in Great Britain
by Amazon